This book is dedicated to James Alvin and Shirley Payne Rankin, their children Alvin, Glenn, Beverly and Alice and their many grandchildren.

3

FOREWORD

When Harry Burroughs approached me about him writing a book about my grandfather, I thought that it was about time someone did. James Rankin has many experiences to share. If you've been around him for more than five minutes, I can guarantee you've heard one or two of them. For years, our family has told him that someone needed to put his stories in print. We're thankful that Harry has finally done so.

As you read through this book, you will learn about Mr. Rankin's humble beginnings, military service and business ownerships. Being his grandson, I can share a few memories that won't make it into the body of this book. Here are some personal stories of the man that I call Pappy.

Growing up, my grandparents had a small family house in Colonial Beach, Virginia. The house was their weekend getaway, as well as a house that the entire family could retreat to. My cousin Ashley and I joined them there one weekend. This was the weekend that he taught us to play

Rummy. Once we got the hang of it, we put a little wager on the game. We bet that if one of us beat him, he would take us to get ice cream. We started playing right after dinner, and thought we'd be getting ice cream within the hour. Well, that didn't happen. He beat us repeatedly.

We lost track of time and kept playing well after my grandmother went to bed. When we finally beat him and looked at the clock, it was two-thirty in the morning. Our hopes for ice cream were dashed until he told us to get our shoes on. A bet was a bet. While we didn't go to a normal ice cream establishment, 7-11 was still open and they had plenty to choose from.

This is not my fondest memory, but if you ask my grandfather, he will beam with pride on this one. We were having dinner out one night, and he and I started trash talking to each other. I don't remember the context, but a challenge was issued as we left the restaurant. It was a race to his vehicle. I have all sorts of excuses. My shoes were untied. I was full from dinner. He started early. Unfortunately, none of my excuses stuck. He beat me. To this day, he will never let me live it down. I refuse to ask for a rematch. I can't handle another loss.

I'm grateful that I'm able to share these memories with you all as you dive into my grandfather's life story. If there's anyone that deserves to have a book written about him, it's Jim Rankin. On behalf of the Rankin family, we want to thank Harry Burroughs for taking the time and doing this for him. We hope you all enjoy reading about his life as much as we have enjoyed being a part of it.

Bryan Kniceley
Warrenton, Virginia
Fall 2023

8

CONTENTS

Chapter 1: Introduction

Francis Fauquier
John Marshall
William "Extra Billy" Smith
John Singleton Mosby
John Quincy Marr
James Alvin Rankin, Sr.

Chapter 2: Midland to Meuse-Argonne

Warrenton Rifles
Clay P. Rankin
War to End All Wars
Meuse-Argonne
John D. Sudduth
Silver Star Recipient

Chapter 3: Home on the Farm

Jimmy Rankin
Great Depression
Franklin D. Roosevelt
Benjamin Pitts
First Army Induction

Chapter 7: Life Well Lived

Northern Virginia Baseball League
Boy Scouts of America
Secretary Robert Gates
Fauquier Sheriffs
Clay Rankin Bridge
Tributes

12

Chapter 1: Introduction

The history of the Commonwealth of Virginia is fascinating. We all remember learning in school that on May 3, 1607, three British ships under the command of Captain Christopher Newport embarked for Jamestown, Virginia.

These ships, the *Constant, Godspeed and Discovery,* had sailed from England 143 days earlier. There were 195 men and boys and 39 sailors who made the perilous journey.

Upon arriving, Captain John Smith established the British Colony of Virginia and it became the fourth English Dominion after England, France, Scotland and Ireland. The colony's motto was: "Behold, Virginia gives the Fourth." Many longtime residents still affectionately refer to the Commonwealth of Virginia as "The Old Dominion."

One hundred and fifty two years later in 1759, Fauquier County, Virginia was established. It had originally been part of a vast English Land Grant held by Sir Thomas Fairfax, who was the 6th Lord Fairfax. Over the years, some of the land was ceded to Prince William County and then the newly created Fauquier. The original inhabitants had been the indigenous people of the Iroquois and Sioux nations.

The county was named after the Lieutenant Governor of Virginia, Francis Fauquier. While there apparently is a legend that Fauquier had won these lands in a poker game, there is no substantive evidence to confirm this claim.

What we do know is that Francis Fauquier was a classical scholar and accomplished economist. He lived a comfortable and prosperous life in the Commonwealth of Virginia.

His father, Dr. Jean Francois Fauquier was a French Huguenot who became incredibly rich after moving to England. He was a protégé of Sir Isaac Newton who is widely viewed as one of the world's greatest mathematicians. He invented calculus.

Jean Francois Fauquier was the Deputy Master of the Royal Mint, he designed cooper coins for King George I and was a Director of the Bank of England. Upon his passing, Dr. Fauquier willed to his son, Francis, 25,000 pounds of bank and South Sea Company stock that would be worth $5 million in today's economy.

Francis Fauquier was sworn-in as Acting Governor and the colony's Chief Administrative Officer on June 5, 1758. This was almost a year before Fauquier County was created. He was the colony's representative for King George II and King George III. He ruled for absentee Governors John Campbell, the 4th Earl of Loudoun and Sir Jeffrey Amherst until his death in Williamsburg on March 3, 1768.

During his tenure, the brutal French and Indian War raged throughout Virginia. There were more than 10,000 colonists who died in this bloody conflict. In an effort to pay for the war, the British Parliament enacted a series of draconian taxes on their American subjects.

These new obligations included the Sugar Tax and Currency Act in 1764 and the infamous Stamp Act the following year. Fauquier was sympathetic to the plight of his constituents. He tried unsuccessfully to convince the British Crown to modify their tax strategy. He then refused to enforce some of the British's government's most egregious policies.

According to the University of Virginia's historical accounts, in 1765, "Fauquier personally defused what could have turned into an ugly incident involving a crowd's confrontation of Virginia's Stamp Agent, George Mercer." Apparently, a crowd of colonists wanted to express their displeasure of the Stamp Act, which taxed documents, playing cards and various forms of paper, by tarring and feathering the Stamp agent.

Governor Fauquier had a number of well known friends throughout the Commonwealth including British Lieutenant Colonel George Washington who owned Ferry Farm near Fredericksburg, Virginia.

Among the notable members of the Virginia House of Burgesses, future U.S. President Thomas Jefferson wrote, "Fauquier was the ablest man to ever serve as Lieutenant Governor of Virginia." The *Encyclopedia Virginia* has concluded, "Fauquier was one of the most popular colonial Lieutenant Governors. His good working relationship with the colony's political leaders and his interest in education earned him respect and praise."

In 1759, the population of Fauquier County was approximately 1,693 taxpayers. It was an agrarian based economy. Tobacco was Virginia's first cash crop and it was sold exclusively in England. This same year, Elias and William Edmonds had a farm near Warrenton that raised Edmonium tobacco.

Fauquier County has been home for a number of prominent citizens. The most famous is John Marshall who was born in a log cabin near present day Midland. He served as a member of the 3rd Virginia Regiment who fought against the British at the Battle of Brandywine. Marshall also survived the brutal winter at Valley Forge in 1778.

After gaining our independence from England, Marshall was elected to the Virginia House of Delegates and Virginia's 13th Congressional District representing Fauquier County in the U.S. House of Representatives during the 6th Congress.

In 1800, John Marshall, whose cousin was Thomas Jefferson, was nominated by then President John Adams as this nation's 4th Secretary of State. Just one-year later, lame duck President Adams appointed John Marshall to serve as our 4th Chief Justice of the United States Supreme Court. There are many historians who believe John Marshall of Midland was our greatest jurist.

A second resident is William "Extra Billy" Smith. While he was not born in Fauquier County, Smith spent many years living on his beloved "Monte Rose" estate in Warrenton. By all accounts, William Smith was a colorful, charismatic and popular leader. He served in the Virginia State Senate, the U.S. House of Representatives, the Confederate

Congress and he was twice elected Governor of the Commonwealth of Virginia.

He earned his nickname "Extra Billy" by submitting invoices to the federal government containing "extra charges" for his contracted mail and stagecoach services.

During the Civil War, Extra Billy Smith was appointed a Colonel of the 49th Virginia Infantry. He fought at the Battle of Fairfax Court House, First Battle of Manassas, Battle of Seven Pines, Battle of Antietam, Battle of Chancellorsville and the Battle of Gettysburg. While he was wounded in several of these battles, he managed to survive the conflagration that was the War Between the States.

Since William Extra Billy Smith never grew tired of public service, he decided to run for a seat in the Virginia House of Delegates. He was elected at the age of 80. He died in 1887 at the age of 89 and is buried in the Hollywood Cemetery in Richmond, Virginia.

A third famous Fauquier County resident is Colonel John Singleton Mosby who was known as the "Gray Ghost." Mosby was born on December 6, 1833 in Powhatan County, Virginia. He entered the University of Virginia in 1852 and was admitted to the Virginia State Bar three years later. During the next six years, he would marry and established several law offices outside of Charlottesville, Virginia.

John Mosby earned his nickname by commanding the Confederate 43rd Battalion Virginia Calvary. Mosby's Raiders were noted for their lightening-quick raids in Fairfax, Loudoun and Prince William counties and their uncanny ability to elude the Union Army.

Colonel Mosby who had a $50,000 Union bounty for his arrest was one of the last Confederate officers to surrender. The adventures of the "Gray Ghost" remain an important part of Virginia history.

Following the end of the Civil War, Mosby reestablished his law practice in Warrenton. Despite great personal risk, John Mosby agreed to serve as the

Virginia campaign manager for Ulysses S. Grant's successful effort to become our nation's 17th President. During the next 20 years, he served as the United States Consul in Hong Kong, South Pacific Railroad lawyer, Special Agent of the Department of the Interior and as a staff attorney for the U. S. Justice Department.

This colorful and once revered Virginian died in Washington, D.C. on May 30, 1916. John Singleton Mosby was 82-years-old and was interred in the Warrenton Cemetery.

The final noteworthy Fauquier County resident is John Quincy Marr. While not as well known as John Marshall, William Smith and John Mosby, Marr lived a life of public service. During his short 36 years of life, he worked for the people of Fauquier County as the Chief Justice of the County Courts, Commonwealth Attorney, Fauquier County Commissioner of the Chancery in the Supreme and County Courts, Fauquier County Sheriff, Mayor of Warrenton and Presiding Judge of the Fauquier County Courts.

On February 3, 1861, 152 delegates were chosen as members of the First Virginia Secession Convention. This was two months before the bombardment of Fort Sumter in South Carolina. The Convention voted 90 to 45 not to secede from the union. John Quincy Marr voted against secession.

On April 17, 1861, the Virginia Secession Convention reconvened and this time voted 88 to 55 to secede from the union. This was five days after Confederate batteries fired on Fort Sumter for 34 consecutive hours. John Marr was not in Richmond for that vote.

Despite his absence, John Quincy Marr was devoted to the Commonwealth of Virginia. He organized the "Warrenton Rifles" militia company and was commissioned as a Lieutenant Colonel in the Confederate Army. In a tragically ironic twist of fate, Colonel Marr, who championed peace and had voted against secession, was killed during a nighttime reconnaissance mission at the Fairfax Court House. John Quincy Marr became the first Confederate officer killed in the bloody Civil War.

It has been estimated that about 1,500 people attended his funeral at the St. James Episcopal Church in Warrenton, Virginia. His remains are interred in the historic Warrenton Cemetery. The Marr house remains a popular dwelling on Culpeper Street in Warrenton.

Today, Fauquier County has a population of about 74,000 people. It contains an area of about 651 square miles. It takes almost an hour to drive from the northernmost portion of Fauquier County to its southern border in Goldvein, Virginia. In terms of size, Fauquier is the 8th largest in the Commonwealth of Virginia. It is bigger than its adjacent counties of Clarke, Culpeper, Loudoun, Prince William, Rappahannock, Stafford and Warren.

My family moved from Water Mill, New York to Fairfax, Virginia in 1965. After completing my university studies, getting my first job and marrying the love of my life, we searched for an affordable place to live. We found a nice townhouse in Manassas, Virginia. We lived there until 1985.

I will never forget the day, my wife excitedly called me while I was working in the Ford House Office Building. She told me she had found a brand new house on a one-acre lot on the D.C. side of Warrenton. After a brief pause, I asked her how far Warrenton was from Capitol Hill? Her response was, "I love the house and you will get used to the commute."

We have never regretted our decision to move to Fauquier County. It is a special place. Our neighbors are kind and compassionate people. From various locations throughout the county, you can view the stunning panorama of beautiful rolling land at the foothills of the Blue Ridge Mountains.

There are dairy and horse farms, fields of growing corn and more than 25 wineries. For those of us who appreciate the open green pastures, Fauquier County has avoided the urban sprawl that has dramatically changed forever the landscape of Fairfax, Loudoun and Prince William counties.

Warrenton is the county seat. It is small town America. Over the years, we have been blessed by locally owned small businesses like Ben and Mary's Steak House, Carter's General Store, Clarke Brothers Gun Shop, Claire's Restaurant, McClanahan's Camera, Messick Farm Market, Pete's Park and Eat and Rankin's Hardware and Rankin's Furniture.

In the past century, there have been many Fauquier County residents who have made valuable contributions to our community as decorated military veterans, successful business owners and public servants. Dr. Ben Carson once said, "Happiness doesn't result from what we get, but from what we give." We owe these men and women a great debt of gratitude for all of their sacrifices.

It is indeed rare to find an individual who have excelled at all three of these categories. This book is about a remarkable man --- a patriot --- who earned two bronze stars for his heroic service during the Korean War, who has owned and operated a number of small businesses throughout Virginia and who served the people of Fauquier County with the highest distinction on the Fauquier County Board of Supervisors. It is a great honor and a humbling experience to write this book about a living legend ---James Alvin "Jim" Rankin, Sr.

Chapter 2: Midland to Meuse-Argonne

Military service to this country has always been a sacred duty for the Rankin family of Midland, Virginia. James Alvin Rankin and his father Clayborne "Clay" Rankin were highly decorated for their military service. Their patriotic service occurred in Korea and Western Europe.

Clay Rankin enlisted in the United States Army at the beginning of 1917 at the age of 18. He was a member of the 2nd Virginia Infantry better known in history as the Warrenton Rifles. The original members of Company C included William G. Bartenstein, James Clatterbuck, Samuel E. Hunsberger, Clarence Moffeth, Raymond Pearson, John W. Rhodes, Clay Rankin and John D. Sudduth.

The 2nd Virginia was combined with the 1st and the 4th Virginia Infantry Regiments. This new regiment became the 116th Regiment or Stonewall's Brigade. It was part of the 29th Infantry Division stationed at Camp McClellan in Anniston, Alabama.

The federal government purchased the land for this training facility in the foothills of the Appalachian Mountains on March 17, 1917 at a cost of $247,000. It consisted of 18,952 acres and was named in honor of Union Major General and 1864 Presidential candidate George B. McClellan.

On September 6, 1917, Private Clay P. Rankin and his "Band of Brothers" arrived at Fort McClellan. This was exactly five months after the United States Congress approved, S. J. Res. 1, a resolution declaring war with Germany. For the next 10 months, these former bookkeepers, clerks, construction workers, cooks, farmers, mechanics, policemen, salesmen and shopkeepers, were trained in bayonet use, gas warfare and small arms fire to kill their enemy.

The goal of the American Expeditionary Forces, under the command of General John Joseph "Black Jack" Pershing, was to stop the forward movement of the Axis Powers and restore peace in Europe. In 1917, the major allied powers were Belgium, the British Empire, France, Italy, Japan and the United States.

The forces of evil were Austro-Hungary, Bulgaria, Germany and the Ottoman Empire.

On May 28, 1918, American troops for the first time fought to defend foreign soil at the Battle of Cantigny, France. There were 318 U.S. soldiers killed. In total, the American Expeditionary Forces were engaged in 13 official military campaigns on the Western Front.

On June 15, 1918, the 116th Regiment embarked from Hoboken, New Jersey on the *U. S. S. Finland.* This ship had previously been an American flagged ocean cruise liner. Their destination was Saint Nazaire, France. Aboard this ship were Clay P. Rankin, Preston H. Craun, Strother M. Corbin, John D. Sudduth, Daniel W. Payne, Bernard and Richard Allison, Raymond G. Pearson and Clarence E. Moffeth.

Twelve days after leaving New Jersey, they arrived at Saint Nazaire. This port city is 274 miles southwest of Paris and nearly 700 miles from the Western Front. Their arrival was a huge lift to the

Allied forces who had been fighting in the "War to End All Wars" since July 28,1914.

It was on that fateful day Archduke Franz Ferdinand, the heir to the Austro-Hungarian Empire, and his wife Sophie was assassinated in Sarajevo. This was the spark that lit the fires of a World War. Ironically, the Duke's last words were, "It is nothing."

The mere presence of these American "doughboys" was a cause for celebration. It instilled a genuine hope these American troops would end the war's stalemate and produce an Allied victory. The term doughboy was first used in our Civil War. It apparently referred to the brass buttons on a soldier's uniform belonging to an infantryman. It is a Yorkshire idiom meaning, "someone has no money."

As one of the doughboys, Clay Rankin carried 200 rounds of ammunition, two cans of corned beef, 6 boxes of army hardtack biscuits and a one-quart canteen. He was also given a medal helmet, Olive Drab Green shirt and pants, leggings, trench coat and shoes, haversack, sewing and shaving kits, soap dish, mess kit, entrenching tool, wire cutters, gas mask, rifle belt, bayonet, Springfield .30 caliber rifle and .45 caliber pistol.

What he would face was a well trained and experience fighting force that were adept at killing Americans, British and French soldiers with airplanes, artillery, flamethrowers, machine guns, poison gas, tanks and submarines. Of all of these merchants of death, the most feared was mustard gas. This weapon produced a yellow or brown mist and to those troops without a working gas mask, it smelled like garlic or onions. In some cases, there was no odor at all.

During the Great War, there were 91,000 troops whose deaths were directly attributed to gas attacks. For those who "survived" this experience, they faced a lifetime of suffering including abdominal pain, diarrhea, fever, nausea and vomiting.

After arriving at the Western Front in August of 1918, the brave men of the 116th Infantry occupied trenches in the

Haute-Marne sector of Alsace, France. In World War I, there were 1,547 miles of trenches. These shelters were about 9 feet deep and 3 to 6 feet wide. Trenches were never dug in a straight line. This was to prevent the enemy from firing straight down the line.

The comforts provided to the troops included cold food, no privacy or showers, 4 to 6 foot deep trench toilets, hordes of bugs, various diseases and thousands of hungry rats to share their sleeping beds in the mud.

Like most troops, Pvt. Clay Rankin must have been horrified when he looked out of his trench to what was called "No Man's Land." During the Great War, these are the lands that separated the Allied and Axis troops.

Due to constant artillery shelling, much of the Western Front had been denuded. There were no living trees, dozens of 100 foot wide and 40 foot deep mine craters, miles of barbed wire, land mines, contaminated soil and water, dead horses and human corpses and wounded soldiers. To Clay Rankin, it must have been like a scene from a horror movie.

It was here on the Western Front where young soldiers like Clay Rankin, John Sudduth and Sam Hunsberger were willing to fight and kill an enemy they didn't know or had any reason to hate. They were ready to make the ultimate sacrifice for the United States of America.

In an effort to end this seemingly endless bloody conflict, General Pershing decided to secretly move 1.2 million American troops to the Meuse-Argonne Forest. This would become the largest land offensive in United States military history. It would be an epic fight been American and battle tested troops of the Imperial German Army.

Among those who faced the Germans for the first time were Pvt. Clay Rankin and the other members of the 116th Regiment. Prior to the first attack, an Army Infantry Private from Mississippi said it was, "As though the heavens were weeping over the sacrifices of so many lives that was so soon to be made."

At dawn on Thursday, September 16, 1918, 5,000 pieces of American artillery bombed the German troops for six consecutive hours. For the 450,000 soldiers who were the target of these shells it must have been terrifying. At the end of this barrage, 600,000 Americans attacked the German lines. It was the deadliest battle in the history of the United States Army.

For members of the 116th Infantry, they would wait and listen for the whistle blown by their leaders telling them it was time to go "over the hill" from their trenches and fight the enemy in No Man's Land. Private Clay Rankin had a different important assignment. He was chosen for one of the most dangerous jobs. For the rest of the battle, he would be a messenger who delivered vital information to other American commanders.

During the Meuse-Argonne campaign, Clay Rankin faced death every day. The battlefield stretched 20-miles from the Meuse River to the Argonne Forest. The weather was abysmal with constant rain, cold river mists and flooded trenches.

With each step, Clay knew his life could be lost by an overhead German Gothas, a hidden machine gun, an unexploded ordinance, gas or even friendly fire. The Germans desperately wanted to kill all messengers because they knew the information they carried could change the outcome of the battle. Yet, somehow, Pvt. Clay Rankin survived. He carried out his missions. He likely saved many American lives because he was an outstanding messenger.

His son, James Alvin Rankin remembers that, "His father had a strong sense of patriotic pride which rubbed off onto him." His dad, "Went through enemy lines where he said no other man could have gotten through." According to his draft registration card, Clay Rankin was 5'4 and weighed 168 pounds. Jim Rankin also added, "He told us how the enemy was always looking for him at night when he hid under brush piles but they didn't find him."

Like all American troops, Clay Rankin not only had to fear the Germans but in September 1918, a new silent demon invaded the battlefield. A second wave of the deadly Spanish Flu arrived along the Western Front. While the symptoms of most influenza gave their victims aches, fever, headaches and a sore throat, this powerful strain produced massive bleeding, trouble breathing and affected patients would have their skin turn blue.

In the United States, 105 million Americans were infected by the Spanish Flu and between 500,000 to 800,000 died. On the European Western Front, this horrible disease killed 15,849 U.S troops in France and 30,000 in stateside military camps.

While it is unclear whether Pvt. Rankin was ever infected by the Spanish flu, many of his brothers were victims. Sgt. Norvel Preston Clotfelter of Missouri wrote, "Felt pretty sick. Had not time to find place to sleep so slept in mud last night. Went for chow AM. So sick coming back went to see the doctor. He gave me some medicine and got me off duty. Lay in dry shed with high fever and chills in the evening. Slept none. Rained nearly all night."

Somehow Clay Rankin --- a farmer from Midland, Virginia --- managed not to be killed by the Germans or Spanish Flu. Unfortunately, he could not avoid being gassed during his assignments. For his heroism, he was recommended to receive a Distinguished Service Cross, Silver Star and an Italian War Cross.

When the 47-days of fighting ended on November 11, 1918, the U.S. Army's Mortuary Affairs Service tallied up the dead. The 29th Division suffered terrible losses at the Battle of Meuse-Argonne. In total, 29 officers and 447 men were killed and 92 officers and 2,303 men were wounded. These casualties represented about 30 percent of the division. In addition, there were 1,644 troops including Clay Rankin who were victims of a poison gas attack.

Among those who paid the ultimate sacrifice for freedom were 32 sons of Fauquier County. This nation must long remember the heroism of Carrington E.

Bailey, Benjamin S. Beverly, Alex Boteler, James Earl Boteler, Wilie S. Brown, Strother M. Corbin, Hugh H, Corum, John S. Dale, Edward Diggs, McKinley Dodd, Herbert L. Foster, G.A. Golden, Jefferson Gordon, Newton Lee Gray, James S. Hall, Kenny Heflin, John R. Hicks, Samuel Edward Hunsberger, Joseph W. Isenberg, Clyde Kane, John A. Kendall, Maury M. Lake, Frank Menefee, John William Moore, James W. Newman, John L. O'Brien, Charles F. Payne, Miller Riley, Albert O. Sudduth, John D. Sudduth., George Bailey Smith and Eugene Wilburn.

One of the most famous names on that list was Corporal John D. Sudduth of Warrenton, Virginia. He was the youngest and last county resident to die in battle during the Meuse-Argonne offensive on October 23, 1918. He was killed by machine gun fire during an attack on the Molleville Farm in France.

Some months after his passing, his older sister Eva Sudduth submitted to *The Fauquier Democrat* a beautiful tribute to her brother. Her words were moving:

Somewhere in the Argonne Forest
Far across the deep blue sea
Sleeps there within a silent grave,
One who is very dear to me.

Dearest, John, how I miss you,
This world will never know,
If tears could bring you home,
You would have been here long ago

So now it's all over; 'Over there,'
And the world's great battle is over
Our dearest heroes now are
Marching home
But not my soldier brother.

Killed in action --- that awful blow
Has stamped my heart with pain
And every day it seems as though
I look for you in vain.
Yes, in the great beyond some day,

After my work on earth is over,
I will then stand face to face
With my angel soldier brother.

The poem was signed: "By his
devoted sister, Eva." John Sudduth was
originally buried in the Meuse-Argonne
American Cemetery in France. His body

was exhumed and reinterred in the Warrenton Cemetery. Eva Sudduth O'Brien passed away on March 12, 1940.

The last surviving World War I veteran from Fauquier County was Sergeant First Class Edward E. "Eddie" Strother, Sr. of Delaplane. He died on April 4, 1997 at the age of 102. The inscription on his tombstone in the Leeds Episcopal Church Cemetery simply reads: Veteran of World War I: Farmer. Counselor to Many.

On November 12, 1918, General Pershing issued General Order No. 232. It said, in part, "You will long be remembered for your stubborn, resistance of your progress, you storming of obstinately defended machine gun nests. Your heroic resistance in the face of counter-attacks supported by powerful artillery fire. For more than a month, you fought your way slowly through the Argonne, through the woods and over hills west of the Meuse." The greatest killer of troops on both sides was massive artillery fire.

This was the battle that ended the Great War but the butcher's bill was staggering. Between 1915 and 1918, 68,176,000 soldiers participated in the war. There were almost 10 million killed and more than 20 million wounded. For the American Expeditionary Forces, there were 53,402 of our troops who perished on the battlefield and 192,483 were wounded.

Pvt. Clay Rankin was a witness to this calamitous destruction. What he saw is something no person should ever see. It was horrific. The now eerily quiet Western Front was filled with mangled bodies of man and beast, abandoned artillery and machine guns and piles of discarded ammunition, bayonets and guns. For the first time since he arrived on the battlefield, Clay Rankin could hear the birds singing and the sweet sound of silence.

Foreign news correspondents reported, "For the first time, men stood up straight in the open with nothing to fear. They built campfires for the first time. They took off their boots, dried their socks and warmed their chilled fingers." It was almost winter in France.

Captain Harry Truman of Independence, Missouri was the Commander of Battery B, 129th Field Artillery, 35th Division. He recalled that on the night of November 11, 1918, "All the men in the French battery became intoxicated as a result of a load of wine. Every single one of them had to march to my bed and salute and yell, 'Vive President Wilson. Vive le Capitaine D'Artillerie Americain."

This popular Captain became the 33rd President of the United States 16 years later. In the White House, it was well known that President Truman was no fan of tea or wine but he did enjoy a shot of Old Grand Dad bourbon as part of his morning routine.

On December 8, 1918, Pvt. Clay Rankin wrote a letter to his father, Preston Baylor Rankin from France. It was printed in *The Fauquier Democrat.* In part, the letter said, "I will try and write you a few lines this beautiful Sabbath day. These few lines leaves me feeling fine and dandy. I guess you are fixing up for Christmas. The French girls are awful pretty and France is noted for plenty of wine and they come around with the bottle and gee, but that wine is fine. "

"Well Pa, as news is getting scarce I will have to stop for this time. Wishing you all a Merry Christmas and a Happy New Year. Love and kisses to mother and sisters and you. Your loving son. Private Clay P. Rankin. " In 1918, Clay had seven sisters and two brothers living in Fauquier County.

It wasn't until May 19, 1918 that Clay Rankin and his band of 116th Regiment brothers left St. Nazaire, France. Their destination on *The U.S.S. Matsonia* was Newport News, Virginia. This was 179 days after the last shot was fired and the Armistice was declared. It must have been a painfully long wait for the Rankin family.

The *Matsonia* finally arrived at the port of Newport News on Tuesday, May 20, 1919. Virginia Governor Westmoreland Davis and Richmond Mayor George Ainslie greeted the victorious troops. *The Fauquier Democrat* reported, "Virginia veterans, men who met and defeated the flower of the German Army, hove in sight. Men and boys went mad. Women forgot themselves pounding each other on the back. Here and there along the line of march a woman dashed from the crowd leaped at the neck of a bronzed hero and without stopping a second, caught steps with the troops and continued on the way to camp."

This was almost two years after Clay Rankin had left his beloved family and home in Midland, Virginia. He had survived but he would be afflicted for the result of his life by the after effects of mustard gas. While his son, James A. Rankin is unaware that he suffered from the effects of "Shell Shock," 250,000 doughboys suffered from this illness we now call Post Traumatic Stress Disorder.

Ironically, at the end of the war, the Western Front had hardly moved during the four years of bloody conflict. The world's greatest hope was a lasting peace. Sadly, it lasted less than two decades when Japan invaded Manchuria, China in 1931.

During the First World War, 6,300 Distinguished Service Crosses and 661 Silver Stars were awarded to members of the United States Army. These awards are considered the second and third-highest military decorations given for valor. An Act of Congress established these awards in 1918. One of the recipients was Clayborne Preston Rankin of Midland, Virginia.

His citation for the Silver Star reads: "For gallantry in Action. Displayed remarkable courage and devotion to duty. 11th October 1918, in the front line through heavy-machine gunfire when it was considered impossible for any one to get through."

Clay Rankin also received the Italian War Cross: This citation reads: "For gallantry in action north of Samogneux, France, 11 October 1918 in carrying important messages under enemy fire, recommended for the Distinguished Service Cross."

During the Great War, the German Army destroyed the entire town of Samogneux. The devastation was so complete the French Government decided not to rebuild the community. It is known as the "Village that Died for France."

According to James Alvin Rankin, his father, Clay Rankin, had also been nominated to receive the Medal of Honor that is our nation's highest decoration for soldiers who display extraordinary heroism. Sadly, this did not occur because of bureaucratic incompetence.

It is interesting to note at least three Americans who served as messengers in World War I were given the Medal of Honor. They performed the exact mission of Clayborne Preston Rankin. Two of them, Pvt. Robert Lester Blackwell of Hurdle Mills, North Carolina and Private First Class Parker F. Dunn of Albany, New York were killed trying to deliver their messages.

A third recipient was 1st Lieutenant George Price Hayes of El Reno, Oklahoma. During the Battle of the Marne, "During unprecedented artillery bombardment by the enemy. Hayes' line of communication was destroyed. He immediately set out to establish contact with the neighboring post of command. Seven horses were shot out from under him and he was severely wounded." George Hayes died in 1978.

For Clay Rankin, who was now 23-years-old, it was time to resume his life on a small farm in Fauquier County. He would marry his wife, Naomi Sally Smith, on July 6, 1921. They have seven children including Preston, Katheryn, Mattie, William, Thomas, James and Charles Rankin. While it was backbreaking work, farming was a vast improvement over being shot at by German soldiers.

It would have been a great honor to meet him. Each Veterans Day, I reflect on the sacrifices my own family made to this great country. In the future, I will also remember the heroic sacrifices of Clay Rankin and his son, James Alvin Rankin. I also try to obtain a poppy from the American Legion or the Veterans of Foreign Wars.

Finally, I re-read Colonel John McCrae's famous World War I poem. The words of this Canadian physician are deeply moving.

"In Flanders Fields the poppies blow Between the crosses, row on row, That mark our place; and in the sky The larks, still bravely singing, fly Scarce heard amid the guns below. We are the dead. Short days ago We lived, felt dawn, saw sunset glow, Loved, and were loved, and now we lie in Flanders fields."

Pvt. Clay Preston Rankin was an American hero. He served with the highest distinction during the biggest, deadliest, most important and last major battle of the War to End All Wars.

Chapter 3: Home on the Farm

On January 16, 1931, James Alvin Rankin was born in Alexandria Hospital at the corner of Duke and Washington Streets. It was the coldest day of the year with an outside temperature of minus 12 degrees Celsius with about two inches of snow on the ground. "Jimmy" was the fourth son of Clay and Naomi Rankin.

He shares his birthday with a number of famous people including award winning actress and singer Ethel Merman, racecar superstar A.J. Foyt and one of country music's most beloved artists, Ronnie Milsap. On his birthday, there was a Jumbo Sale at Kirson's Department Store in Warrenton, Billy the Kid was playing at the Pitts Fauquier Theatre and one of the most popular elixirs for the common cold was Father John's Medicine. It is still available today.

After being discharged from the Alexandria hospital, Jimmy Rankin joined his growing family of seven-year old Katheryn, five-year old Mattie, three-year old William and 16-month old Thomas

Rankin. Together they lived on a farm in Falls Church, Virginia.

In 1931, Herbert Hoover was the 31st President of the United States, John Garland Pollard was Virginia's Governor, the U.S. Senators were Carter Glass and Claude Swanson and the local 8th District Congressman was Howard Worth Smith. Jimmy Rankin was born 15-months after the beginning of the largest and worst economic depression in United States history.

According to one of America's well-known social commentator and humorist, Will Rogers, "Our whole depression was brought on by gambling, not in the stock market alone but in borrowing and going into debt all just to make some easy money quick."

Prior to October 1929, millions of Americans had invested their hard earned dollars in the U.S. Stock Market. There was even a Warrenton branch of the New York Stock Exchange known as Wright, Slade and Company. It was a period known as the "Roaring Twenties," where nearly every American believed they could become rich. Fedora hats, flapper dresses, jazz music and speakeasies were widely popular. There was a sense that good times were here to stay.

Sadly, dreams of enormous wealth came crashing down on October 29, 1929. This day became known as "Black Tuesday." Between 1929 and 1932, the U.S. Stock market lost 90 percent of its financial value. American investors that included clerks, doctors, farmers, factory workers, teachers and shopkeepers lost a staggering $60 billion dollars. Millions also lost their jobs, homes and hope for the future.

During the Great Depression that lasted from October 1929 to December 1941, our unemployment rate reached 24.7 percent, the U.S. Gross National Product fell by 26.7 percent and there were more than 2 million homeless people in the United States. These folks were forced to live with relatives or shacktowns known as Hoovervilles. There was widespread misery throughout the country. The expression of the day was, "Brother Can You Spare A Dime."

Farmers were particularly hurt in the Great Depression. In a blink of an eye, crop prices tanked, land values fell and many farms were worth less than the loans the banks held. There were dairy farmers in Iowa and Nebraska who dumped their milk products in ditches in a desperate attempt to increase demand.

There was a massive heat wave in the Midwest in 1934. For nearly a month, farmers faced temperatures higher than 100 degrees. There were dust storms and soon a growing Dust Bowl throughout this region.

There were 2.4 million people living in the Commonwealth of Virginia in 1931. Of this total, thousands of residents were working and making a living on 170,610 farms. The prices for farm products dropped to historic levels. Farm income was cut in half. In 1932, a bushel of corn was selling for as little as 8 to 10 cents. Americans were burning corn for heat because it was cheaper than coal.

Life Magazine concluded, "Daily life on the farm during the Great Depression was a tough life full of hard work and few luxuries. Many farmers had a terrible time due to overproduction and plunging farm prices."

As a result of this catastrophe, 750,000 farms in the United States were bankrupted and lost to bank foreclosures. Farmers were forced to beg for more time to pay their loans or seek menial jobs. The act of bartering clothing for canned fruits and vegetables became popular.

The first local mention of the Great Depression appeared in the opinion section of the November 30, 1929 edition of *The Fauquier Democrat.* The article was entitled, "Hot Air Cannot Stop Hard Times." It was a direct challenge to President Herbert Hoover who proved to be ill equipped to lead this country during our worst economic collapse.

Hoover had been one of the first graduates of Stanford University in California. After receiving his degree, a British mining company hired him. Hoover became rich as a mining engineer in China and Australia. His public service included Chairman of the Commission for the Relief in Belgium, Director of U.S.

Food Administration and US Secretary of Commerce. Prior to his landslide victory as President in 1928, he had never been elected to serve in government.

President Hoover's initial response to the stock market crash was to ignore it. When that strategy failed, he decided it was not the job of a President to interfere in the national economy. Hoover famously said, "Economic depression cannot be cured by legislative action or Executive pronouncements."

Clay Rankin never invested in the U.S. Stock Market nor was he a fan of Herbert Hoover. Clay simply did not have any extra money to speculate or gamble. Every dollar was needed to put food on the table and care for his family.

Fauquier County farmers worked together to plant and harvest crops. Unlike office jobs, farming is not a five-day, 40-hour workweek. There were no summer vacations for the Rankin family. According to Jimmy Rankin, "We didn't start going to school until January. We worked on the farm, didn't go to school until all the crops were in."

Cows cannot milk themselves and weeds must be plowed or pulled by hand. It was backbreaking work especially for someone, like Clay Rankin, who suffered from the effects of World War I mustard gas poisoning. His son, Jimmy Rankin recalled, "He was burned up with illness. He thought he would die at any time." There were frequent visits to the Rankin house by Dr. George Davis who founded the first hospital in Fauquier County in 1925 and faithfully cared for his patients for over 60 years.

Nevertheless, it had to be gratifying to Clay Rankin to see his crops planted in the spring result in a bountiful harvest in the fall. The fruits of the Rankin family efforts were picked, canned and enjoyed all year. Over the years, the family planted corn, hay, tomatoes and wheat. Our first President, George Washington remarked, "Agriculture is the most helpful, most useful and most noble employment of man."

While I have never lived on a farm, I spent a number of years in a farming community. Our home in Water Mill, New York was surrounded on three sides by commercial potato fields. Each summer, I would help my friends, the Zaluski's, harvest their cucumbers, green beans and potatoes. It was a family operated farm with three generations of Zaluski's doing the work. They had no extra money to hire migrant pickers. My reward for working was cold pizza and warm cokes.

I would arrive home each summer night exhausted. Each of my hands was yellowish green, my eyelids were caked with dirt and I desperately needed a hot shower. While I loved the farming life, it was hard and I was happy to see the new school year start after Labor Day. I have never forgotten this family's incredible work ethic and their love of the land.

Clay Rankin loved his leased land but it was a hard life. According to Jimmy Rankin, "I don't know of anyone who could have been poorer than we were. Mama said we may not have much, but we'd always have clean clothes, kerosene for our lamps and plenty of food." He also mentioned the Rankin home didn't have electricity or a telephone. They used a well-built clean outhouse, which likely had a copy of the Sears Roebuck catalog.

While the Rankin family never had a lot of money, they never asked for a government handout. They placed their faith in hard work and in God. They had a "victory garden" long before they became popular. They sold some of their grain and hay crops and milked about ten cows in a "50-50 arrangement" with the owner of the farm. Jimmy's family sold cream from the fresh milk to generate a meager income.

Sundays were always the Lord's Day. This meant each member of the Rankin family would travel together to the Midland Church of the Brethren. This house of worship had been established in 1883 and its first minister was Rev. Solomon Snell.

Its original membership was largely comprised of farmers who had moved to Fauquier County from the Shenandoah Valley. The Midland Church of the Brethren was the first new congregation in Northern Virginia. The church mission is, "Continuing the Work of Jesus. Simply. Peacefully. Together." It wasn't until 1953 when the church had its first full-time resident pastor with the selection of Rev. John Dettra.

The Rankin families have been members of the Midland Church for generations. It is here where they were married, worshipped, enjoyed fellowship and food and received the spiritual guidance needed to face the Great Depression, droughts, floods, World Wars and personal tragedies. The church has always played a key role in their lives and the Church of the Brethren Cemetery became their final resting place.

On those occasions when the Rankin family went to the Town of Warrenton, Clay Rankin could buy a new truck tire at the Firestone Store for less than $30. He could shop at the local Great Atlantic and Pacific Tea Company (A&P) and pay 33 cents for a pound of bacon, 25 cents for 11 pounds of 8'Oclock coffee and 21 cents for two pounds of lard.

He could visit Ullman's on Culpeper Street. This department store had opened in 1845. The first owner Abraham
Rinsberg was a Jewish German peddler. Upon his passing, the store was owned

and was operated by daughter, Caroline Rinsberg Ullman and her son Joseph until it was sold in 1960.

Ullman shoppers could find an array of products for all ages. The store's long time slogan was, "Sell everything to everybody." For instance in 1931, work shirts were sold for 59 cents, men's shoes for $2.89, a ladies dress was $3 and winter coats were $4.49.

During this same year, dozens of Fauquier County farms were sold at public or trustee sales. In 1920, there were 2,640 farms in the county. This represented 379,779 acres of farmland valued at $17.1 million. A decade later, there were only 1,787 farms in the county. These 354,941 acres were worth $16 million.

As a result of the Great Depression and a severe drought, 853 farms in Fauquier County were sold or foreclosed on by the local banks. This was a loss of not only dozens of family farms but also nearly 25,000 acres of land. There was great misery down on the farm.

On January 1, 1931, a young farm girl from Reedley, California wrote to First Lady Lou Henry Hoover. This letter could have been written by millions of Americans. In her correspondence Miss Martha Fast stated, "I am a poor girl and haven't many clothes. I have to wear the same dress almost every time I go somewhere." She then inquired whether the First Lady had any discarded clothes and, "If you happen to know anyone that has some, please remember I would be so happy to receive some."

Less than a week later, a Secretary to Mrs. Hoover responded, "She finds it impossible to be of any help at all. I am sorry I do not know of any clothing just now which she does not need." Two months later, Arkansas resident Mike Clark submitted a letter to *The Fauquier Democrat* about the "Hoover Prosperity." He ended his letter by stating; "Write if you hear of any relief from this government coming down this way. I am willing to be a Republican for a few weeks if that will help any." Sadly, it was clear, needy and starving Americans weren't going to get any help from the Hoover White House.

On November 8, 1932, the chickens come home to roost for Herbert Hoover. Due to his unwavering unwillingness to use the federal government to help fellow Americans during the Great Depression, voters repudiated his policies and denied him a second term as President. When all the ballots were counted, New York Governor Franklin Delano Roosevelt (FDR) was elected our 32nd President.

FDR received 22.8 million votes, 472 electoral votes and carried 42 of 48 states. By contrast, Herbert Hoover somehow received 15.7 million votes, 59 electoral votes and carried six states. In Virginia, Roosevelt received 203,979 or 70 percent of the vote and he carried every one of the state's 99 counties except for Floyd County. Farmers in Fauquier County soundly rejected Herbert Hoover. He received 379 votes out of a total of 2,378 cast. This was about 15 percent of all ballots. Clay and Naomi Rankin were proud members of the Democratic Party. They placed their faith in Franklin Roosevelt and were not disappointed in his policies.

President Roosevelt was not shy about using the federal government to revitalize the economy. Among FDR's efforts were: the creation of the Civilian Conservation Corps that hired 250,000 unemployed men to work in rural projects; the Agricultural Adjustment Administration to increase farm product prices, the National Labor Relations Act to allow collective bargaining and the Social Security Act of 1935 to provide a safety net to help millions of Americans from poverty.

In Fauquier County, $67,000 in federal government relief and emergency funds was distributed. Approximately, 1,368 residents benefited from this program. Sadly, this was only 7 percent of county residents. Despite FDR's best efforts, the Great Depression persisted in causing pain and anguish.

This dramatically changed on December 7, 1941. On that infamous day, the Imperial Japanese Navy attacked U.S. military installations and ships at Pearl Harbor, Hawaii. 2,403 American citizens were murdered and 19 U.S. naval vessels either sunk or were damaged. As a result of the attack, the Japanese had awaking an industrial and military giant.

The U. S. Congress declared war on Japan the next day. Immediately after this unforgivable Japanese assault, thousands of Americans rushed to enlist in our armed forces. Every man between the ages of 18 to 65 was required to register for the draft. Among those who registered was 43-year-old Clay Preston Rankin. At the time, he and his family were living on the C. E. Ruffner's Farm in Warrenton, Virginia. Due to his advanced age and medical condition, Clay Rankin was not inducted into our military.

Instead, he was assigned to work at the U.S. Naval Torpedo Station in Alexandria, Virginia. Over the course of the war, this facility was responsible for the manufacturing and maintenance of thousands of torpedoes. It also served as a munitions storage area for the East Coast Submarine Fleet of the United States. During the Second World War, United States submarines firing 14,748 torpedoes destroyed 4,112 enemy merchant ships.

In December of 1941, Jimmy Rankin was 10-years-old and he was no longer the youngest member of the Rankin family, His brother Charles Rankin had been born on September 11, 1934. It was a scary time to grow-up in America.

The home radio provided nightly updates on the various battles occurring in Europe, North Africa and on distant unfamiliar islands in the Pacific. Fauquier families were praying for their loved ones overseas. No one wanted to receive a telegram from Western Union located on Main Street in Warrenton.

While the Rankin's did have a battery operated farm radio, the children were far too busy working on the farm to sit down and listen to this wireless gizmo. Batteries were expensive and daylight was short. It is likely that Clay Rankin first heard about the vicious attack on Pearl Harbor on his radio and he may have listened to some of President Roosevelt's famous "fireside chats."

Every county home was required to blackout their windows and the fear of being attacked was palpable. Members of the Fauquier County government stoked those fears by scheduling almost monthly blackouts. Citizens were told it was against the law to use their house lights or even candles during these drills. In the Town of Warrenton, streetlights were not lit and motorists had to use their dimmer or brake lights. Those citizens who failed to obey faced fines and potential jail time.

During most American wars, the constitutional rights of citizens are frequently ignored. World War II was no exception. As a result of edits issued by the Fauquier County Rationing Board almost all products were limited in their distribution. These included automobiles, canned foods, coal, gasoline, meat, nylons, rubber, shoes, silk and sugar. Each family got a coupon book specifying how much and when a product could be purchased.

Fauquier farmers were told, "Everyone who slaughters livestock after March 31, 1943 for the purpose of selling meat must register with the County War Board and secure a permit." During the war, horsemeat became a staple for many Fauquier families because most beef and pork were reserved for our troops. The federal government even banned sliced bread. This was an attempt to conserve steel. There was such a howl of protest about this foolish idea that the ban was lifted after only two months.

In the May 27, 1943 edition of *The Fauquier Democrat,* citizens were told, "The gasoline situation is very critical and everyone is urged not to use their cars and trucks unless it is vitally important." Gasoline was strictly limited to three gallons a week. This made it extremely difficult for farmers to plant, cultivate and bring their crops to market.

In an effort to provide a small amount of income for Fauquier County residents, the State of Virginia initiated a scrap campaign. The first such campaign occurred in September 1942. Among the items the state was seeking to collect were bathtubs, batteries, beds, electric appliances, junked farm machinery, keys, pots and pans, roller skates, sleds, stoves and vacuum cleaners. It was a giant but serious scavenger hunt.

The entire Rankin family, including Jimmy, participated in this patriotic effort.

What 11-year old doesn't want to collect metal junk to help their family. As a result of the efforts of hundreds of Fauquier County families, 264,000 pounds of scrap metal was collected. This impressive haul was transported to local junk dealers and used for bullets and guns for our soldiers. In 1942, the value of this scrap was 40 cents per pound. What the county citizens collected was worth about $105,600 that was distributed to those who found the items.

The local newspapers were the forums used by the federal, state and local governments to sell War Bonds and stamps. The constant advertisements had catchy expressions like: Buy War Bonds Before Its Too Late, For Freedom's Sake and Keep Him (Nazi with bayonet) Off Your Streets. In Fauquier County there were seven major funding raising efforts. They were promoted at dances, rallies and shows. They were highly successful and millions of dollars were raised in Fauquier County for our troops.

Nearly, 80 million Americans spent $61 billion on War Bonds and stamps. You could purchase them at the Post

Office on Main Street in Warrenton, most retail stores and even the Pitts Fauquier Theatre. During most films, Hollywood celebrities such as Joan Bennett, Bing Crosby, Cary Grant, Bob Hope and Roy Rogers spoke of the vital need for Americans to buy War Bonds. In September of 1942, the Pitts Fauquier Theatre manager, T.I. Martin, offered one free ticket for the immediate purchase of one War Bond.

For many Fauquier County children, like Jimmy Rankin, they do not remember the war period fondly. There were a number of draconian measures that produced sadness in the community. The Gold Cup and the Warrenton Firemen's Carnival were cancelled. Instead of celebrating the holidays, county leaders prohibited Christmas lights in Warrenton and even cancelled Santa Claus' annual Pre-Christmas visit. Authorities went so far as to outlaw *The Fauquier Democrat's* annual Christmas Special Edition.

These were terrible ideas. Even the troops themselves celebrated Christmas on the front. These events had for years brought the county together and they produced a brief period of happiness to a community that desperately needed it. Instead of celebrating, the order of the day was, "Work, Fight or Go To Jail." Sheriff Woolf prepared a list of able-bodied non-workers and threatened them with six months in his jail.

In his free time, Jimmy Rankin enjoyed his visits to the local ponds and streams, fishing with his brother Charlie and playing baseball. In the 1940's, this was America's favorite pastime. There were pick-up baseball games with his brothers and neighborhood kids. If you had a few dollars you could buy a baseball bat for 95 cents, baseballs for $1.10, baseball shoes for $1.98 and a baseball glove for $2 from the local department store or the Sears and Roebuck catalog

By working hard, Jimmy Rankin was able to save a little money to pay for his favorite pursuit, going to the Pitts Fauquier Theatre at 65 Main Street in Warrenton. Fredericksburg businessman Benjamin Thomas "Bennie" Pitts had owned this theatre since 1935. In the early 1950's there was also a Pitts Drive-

In Theatre on Bear Wallow Road in Warrenton.

Bennie Pitts was a fascinating man. He established Pitts Enterprises in 1909 at the age of 15. He was a consummate entrepreneur. During the course of his life he owned 37 theatres and opera houses. In 1937, his chain of theatres included Berryville, Culpeper, Emporia, Fredericksburg, Front Royal Leesburg, Manassas, Orange, Richmond, Suffolk, Warrenton, West Point and Charles Town, West Virginia. Benjamin Pitts was also a public servant as a member of the Fredericksburg City Council and Virginia State Senate.

This was the "Golden Age of Cinema." During the 1940's, the Pitts theatre offered a variety of films. The cost of this entertainment was 11 cents for children and 28 cents for adults. This included the tax. There were 700 seats in the air-conditioned Pitts Theatre. For 20 cents, a patron could buy a bag of hot popcorn and a cold Coke. The theater was constructed using advanced fireproof methods and was always cool during a hot summer day. Sadly, the theatre was segregated with black patrons having to use their own entrance and restrooms. These Americans were unfairly forced sit in the balcony section of the theater.

Benjamin Pitts loved western movies and especially those starring Roy Rogers, Gabby Hayes, Tex Ritter, Wild Bill Elliott and John Wayne. Between 1941 and 1945, Hollywood produced 400 western movies. Many of these were shown to Fauquier County residents. As the war intensified films like Action in the North Atlantic, Across the Pacific, Bataan, Casablanca, Commanders Strike at Dawn, Destination Tokyo, Thirty Seconds Over Tokyo, Thunderbirds, and You're in the Army Now were booked. Each film was preceded by a Newsreel, Sports or Travel feature, or a cartoon or action adventure short like Dick Tracy or Riders of Death Valley.

Benjamin Pitts also embraced new technology. He booked Deep in the Heart of Texas, Gone With the Wind, To the Shores of Tripoli and Wizard of Oz. Each of these films was shown in Technicolor a new process of color cinematography. Apparently, the owner was not a fan of either Walt Disney or Tarzan films. During the entire war, only Dumbo was shown for two days in August of 1942 and despite multiple films the only time Fauquier County residents got to see Johnny Weissmuller on the big screen was March 13, 1942. The film was Tarzan's Secret Treasure.

Jimmy Rankin always loved movies because they were filled with adventure, cowboys, heroes and they were a brief escape from the hard work on the farm and misery Americans were experiencing during the Great Depression. For two hours, Jimmy Rankin could be Roy Rogers, Jimmy Stewart or John Wayne. What teenage boy didn't want to see cowboys or brave American soldiers killing Nazis' or Japanese on battlefields throughout the world?

Benjamin T. Pitts died on July 21, 1964 after an extended illness at the Medical College of Virginia Hospital of Richmond. This hospital was the region's only comprehensive Level I trauma center for burn patients. The Pitts Theatre, which closed on May 12, 1974, was also used for Prohibition meetings, Red Cross rallies and the annual Warrenton High School graduation ceremonies. It was an integral component of social life in Fauquier County.

In 1943, the powerful Fauquier County Rationing Board further limited gasoline consumption by establishing "No Pleasure Driving Rules." The purpose was to prohibit most driving on weekends especially on Sundays. Sheriff Stanley Woolf was instructed to arrest violators. Since Jimmy Rankin was too young to own a car, he hitchhiked to the Pitts Fauquier Theatre

This was a silly rule. Unfortunately, in times of crisis, certain individuals become self-important and have a tendency to abuse their temporary power. The rule did not make it clear what was "pleasure driving" and Sheriff Woolf and his small force of deputies had more important duties than stopping movie fans. During this same period, there was a rabies epidemic raging throughout the county. Thousands of stray dogs were captured and killed. Despite these efforts, there were more than 30 Fauquier County residents who were bitten by rabid canines.

In the 1940's, there were a number of department stores in Warrenton. These included Cornblatt's Department Store, Grayson's, Lerner Brothers and Ullman's Department Store. There were other popular merchants within the community including Blue Ridge Hardware, Jimmie's Market and Rhodes Drug Store.

Jimmy Rankin liked to shop in these stores. Even at an early age, he was a merchant at heart who was fascinated how products were marketed and sold to the public. There was a science to selling especially during the Great Depression. A potential consumer had to be convinced to spend his limited income on products they just couldn't live without. While Jimmy may not have bought a lot of goods, Lerner Brothers, Ullman's and the 5 and 10 cents store were always on his shopping list.

He was a frequent visitor to the Rhodes Drug Store at 77 Main Street in Warrenton. Jimmy wasn't there to buy medicine but to sit at the old fashion lunch counter. It was here where you could buy a hamburger, fries, malt or a sweet tasting coke. It was also the place to buy fishing lures, newspapers and your favorite candy.

In the 1940's, Jimmy Rankin would have been tempted by a cornucopia of sweet treats such as almond joys, bazooka bubble gum, Dot Gum Drops, Fun Dips, Junior Mints or M&M's. These were first given to soldiers as rations during the Spanish Civil War in 1936.

On September 2, 1945, the Japanese government unilaterally surrendered to the Allied forces on the *U.S.S. Missouri.* The Second World War was finally over. Sadly, the evil forces of Germany and Japan had killed 407,300 Americans who had served in the U.S. Army, Coast Guard, Marines and Navy.

Over 2,000 men and women from Fauquier County had served in World War II. There are 97 names on the Wall of the Fauquier Veterans Memorial who made the ultimate sacrifice for freedom. County residents survived Pearl Harbor and fought in every major European and

Pacific battlefield campaign. Among those recognized were Distinguished Service Cross Recipient, U.S. Army 2nd Lt. John W. Molton of Orlean and Silver Star Recipients Army Lt. Colonel George Dickerson of Warrenton, Army Lt. Colonel Clare B. Mitchell of Catlett and Navy Captain Alan R. Montgomery.

At the time of Emperor Hirohito's surrender, Jimmy Rankin was 14-years-old. He had followed each battle of World War II. He had prayed for our soldiers and suffered over the loss of neighbors in far away countries. While the Rankin boys were not old enough to serve during World War II, Jimmy has always had a great love for this country.

He was bitterly disappointed he couldn't have join in this heroic effort to stop the Nazis and Japanese from enslaving the world. One of the major heroes of the war, General of the Army, Douglas MacArthur said, "No man is entitled to the blessings of freedom unless he be vigilant in its preservation." James Alvin Rankin had been ready to risk his life to defend this country.

The Great Depression and World War II were now history. During the war, Fauquier County was never attacked or bombed by Germans or Japanese. The only time residents got to see the enemy was when 100 German prisoners of war were shipped to Fauquier County to work on farms in 1945. With yet another world conflict over, the fundamental question became how could peace in the world be preserved? Sadly, despite the creation of the United Nations in New York City on October 24, 1945, a lasting peace would prove to be short lived.

With the winds of war blowing on the Korean Peninsula, Jimmy Rankin, who was 17-years-old, decided to join the United States Army. He successfully completed basic training at Fort Jackson in Columbia, South Carolina. This base has long served as one of the Army's main production centers for Basic Training.

Prior to his deployment, military authorities discovered that neither of Jimmy Rankin's parents had given written permission for him to enlist as a minor. In his words, "No one had signed for me, so I was sent home." Jimmy may have been given an honorable minor discharge, but he never lost his desire to serve. He was always interested in being part of something bigger than himself.

Chapter 4: Rakkasans

Sunday, June 25, 1950, was an extremely hot and dry day in Warrenton, Virginia. Jimmy Rankin and his family were celebrating the Sabbath. Each member dressed for church and, unlike the godless North Koreans, spent the day in fellowship, prayer and reflection at the Midland Church of the Brethren.

Nearly 7,000 miles away, 75,000 members of the North Korean People's Army poured across the 38th parallel separating the Communist north and the Democratic Republic of South Korea. This was the first military action of the newly declared Cold War. The brutal dictator of North Korea, Kim ll-sung wanted to blatantly violate the 6th Commandant of "Thou shall not kill," by murdering his 20 million freedom loving southern neighbors.

According to U.S. Army Counter Intelligence, "They somehow missed the massive build up of North Korean troops on the border." This grave oversight is considered one of the most serious intelligence failures in U.S. history. Three days after the invasion, North Korean troops seized Seoul the capital of South Korea located 30 miles south of the Demilitarized Zone.

On June 27, 1950, the United Nations Security Council adopted Resolution 83 authorizing UN member states to provide military assistance to South Korea. As a permanent member, the Soviet Union could have vetoed the Resolution. Instead they boycotted the discussion and the vote. At that time, the Republic of China and not the People's Republic of China held a permanent seat in the Security Council.

As a result of this United Nations action, 16 member countries sent troops to fight the North Koreans. The largest contingents of troops were from the United States with 1,789,000, South Korea with 100,000 and Great Britain with 60,000.

After four months of fighting, UN forces had destroyed the bulk of the North Korean Army and the American troops had advanced to the Yalu River that separates North Korea and the People Republic of China. They were unexpectedly met there by 18 divisions of the People's Volunteer Army. Under the genocidal leadership of Mao Tse-Tung, the Chinese Communist government was intent on maintaining a communist state along their border. As a result, 2.3 million Chinese troops crossed into North Korea and inflicted heavy losses on United Nations forces.

The North Koreans also received the encouragement and support of the Soviet Union. In fact, there is historical evidence that it was their murderous dictator Joseph Stalin who had motivated the North Koreans to invade South Korea. The Soviets sent 70,000 fighters and tons of military equipment. It was established, "the Soviets supplied the North Koreans with large quantities of heavy artillery, T'34 tanks, trucks, automatic weapons and 180 new aircraft." During the war, it was common for U.S. F-86 Sabres and Russian MiG-15's to engage in armed battle over the skies of the Korean Peninsula.

On January 5, 1951, James Rankin re-enlisted in the United States Army. Joining the military was an extremely difficult decision. According to Mr. Rankin, "The Brethren are opposed to war. But, I believe as did my father that it was my duty to join the military to protect our country."

He became a proud member of the famous 187th Airborne. He wanted to fight in one of the most dangerous, elite and respected units of the U.S. military. In 2000, Jim Rankin told the *Fauquier Times,* "They gave us a big demonstration and the fellows in the Airborne looked sharp. I said to myself, that's for me." He wanted to be a member of the "best fighting force" and there was a small amount of one-upmanship with his highly decorated father. The nickname of the 187th is Rakkasans. It is a Japanese word meaning, "Falling down umbrella man." The unit's motto is "Let valor not fail."

The 187th was constituted on November 12, 1942 at Camp MacKall in South Pines, North Carolina. They have fought in World War II, Korea, Vietnam, Afghanistan and Iraq. During the Korean

War, the unit earned two Presidential citations and five battle streamers. It was the only airborne regimen to achieve such battle honors.

After his second induction in the U.S. Army, Private James Rankin was sent to Fort Campbell in Kentucky. This facility was built in 1942 and named in honor of the last Whig Governor of Tennessee William Bowen Campbell.

During nine weeks of basic and airborne training at Fort Benning, Jimmy Rankin learned how to jump out of a moving plane, navigate his free fall to earth, properly dispose of his $50 parachute and prepare to deploy for combat. He passed the course with flying colors.

For Jim Rankin, airborne travel was an exhilarating experience. During his jumps, he was always careful but never really scared. The goal was to, "Get in and get out safely." As someone who has never attempted this feat, I remain skeptical of the logic of jumping out of a plane traveling at 126 miles an hour. When Jim Rankin was recently asked,

"Why airborne?" He responded, "It was $50 dollars more a month." It takes a special person, like Jim Rankin, to become a paratrooper.

On March 23, 1951, 3,437 airborne paratroopers of the 187th were dropped 19-miles north of the United Nations front line at the village of Munsan-Ni, South Korea. It was called Operation Tomahawk. These troops were transported on a fleet of C119s (Flying Boxcars) and C-46s. This was the second time during the Korean War that a large of number of troops, anti-tank guns, howitzers, mortars and trucks were successfully dropped into a battle.

The commander of the operation was then Colonel Frank S. Bowen. During his long and outstanding military career, Frank Bowen was awarded two Distinguished Service Crosses, four silver stars, a Legion of Merit and a Bronze Star. He rose to become a Major General in the United States Army.

The objective of this mission was to trap Chinese and North Korean troops at Munsan-Ni between the Han and Imjin

Rivers. Fighting was fierce. The 187th seized its objective of holding a clump of trees perceived to be the enemy's escape route. While some Communists were able to avoid capture, American troops killed many Chinese and North Korean combatants.

When asked about the battle, General Matthew Ridgeway candidly responded, "The purpose of this operation was to kill the enemy." Of the more than 3,000 American paratroopers, only four made the ultimate sacrifice for this country. Operation Tomahawk again demonstrated the effectiveness of airborne troops and it was highly successful in pushing Chinese Communist troops above the 38th Parallel.

After leaving Fort Benning, Georgia, members of the 187th Airborne Regimental Combat Team including Pvt. Jim Rankin boarded the troopship the *USNS Private Joe P. Martinez*. Their destination was Korea and their trip would last about two weeks. Jim Rankin was now officially a proud member of the 11th Airborne Division, 2nd Battalion, Fox Company. I am sure there were many anxious moments on the troopship because all 1,000 passengers were well aware of what had transpired during Operation Tomahawk. Each of their lives was going to be changed forever. They would hear, see and witness horrible events they would never forget.

From May 1951 to July 1953, Private Rankin and then Staff Sergeant Rankin honorably served his country. During these 26 months of service, 16 ½ months were on the ground fighting in Korea. During the remaining 9 1/2 months, he was stationed at the 187th unit headquarters at Camp Chickamauga in Beppu, Japan. Since the United States, under the leadership of General Douglas A. MacArthur, occupied Japan until April 8, 1952, Jim Rankin was credited with World War II service.

Jim Rankin was sent to Korea with his unit on five separate occasions. On these travels, he opined, "We could be in Japan in the morning, and the call would come out. And we would be in Korea by afternoon."

During 1951, Pvt. Jim Rankin and the 187th Airborne fought "all over Korea." This included ongoing engagements with the Chinese and North Koreans near Inchon, Korea that is 25 miles from the South Korean Capitol and in the "Iron Triangle." This area is comprised of Kumhwa Valley, Ponggang and Youngdung-Po. The fighting was always intense and deadly.

When all casualties were counted, the Rakkasans had suffered more losses in Korea than in World War II, Vietnam and the Persian Gulf War combined. In total, 442 Rakkasans had been killed and 1,673 wounded. Ironically, during his early days of fighting, Pvt. Jimmy Rankin received a draft notice from Uncle Sam stating, "You are hereby directed to present yourself for Armed Forces Physical Examination to a Local Board."

Following various battles and engagements in what was being called a "Police Action" in Korea, the 187th Airborne was re-deployed to Camp Chickamauga, Beppu, Japan. While in Japan, about 1,500 POWs held on the Korean Island of Koje-do, decided to attack the United States Army's 2nd Infantry Division that was guarding them. This incident occurred on February 8, 1952. This prison facility had been built to house 38,400 POW's. There were about 80,000 Chinese and North Korean prisoners in 17 overcrowded compounds at the time of the uprising.

Fortunately, order was restored but not before one American soldier was killed and 38 were wounded. As a result, Brigadier General Francis W. Dodd, a West Point graduate, was given command of the prison. Despite this change in leadership, there were almost daily riots and conditions were deteriorating. In an effort to lower tensions, General Dodd agreed to meet with the POW leadership in the camp. For his efforts, the base commander was captured and detained by the Communist on May 6, 1952.

After this brazen act, the perpetuators erected a giant banner that said, "We captured Dodd. As long as our demand will be solve, his safety is secured. It there happens a brutal act such as shooting, his life is in danger."

Their demands for his release included: the admission of all Communist ringleaders to Compound 76 for a strategy conference, the end the screening of prisoners, medical representatives, an end to "voluntary" repatriation and 1,000 sheets of paper. More importantly, they demanded the UN issue a statement stipulating they were responsible for the bloodshed occurring in the camps.

General Mark W. Clark, whose nickname was American Eagle, was the Commander of the United Nations Command in Korea. His initial response was, "Let them keep that dumb son of bitch Dodd, and then go in and level the place." Fortunately for Francis Dodd, the new Acting Base Commander at Koje-do, Brigadier General Charles F. Colson, issued the following statement, "I do admit that there have been instances of bloodshed where many prisoners of war have been killed or wounded by UN Forces. I can assure you that in the future the prisoners of war can expect humane treatment in this camp. There will be no more forcible screenings."

This was a remarkable capitulation. I suspect there are few, if any, other examples of where POW inmates captured the U.S. base commander and then sought and obtain concessions from their captors. This was a major propaganda triumph for the North Koreans. General Mark Clark was angry at the capture, negotiations and outcome of what he described as, "The biggest flap of the war."

While General Dodd was released unharmed after 78 hours of confinement, it was the end of his and General Colson's military careers. At the direction of the United States Command both men were relieved of duty at the prison camp, reduced to the rank of Colonel and forced to retire from the United States Army. There was a review board inquiry into this event but Colonel Dodd was not informed of its existence, not allowed to appear to offer a defense and denied the opportunity to see the final report.

It was under these circumstances that the 187th Airborne including Sgt. Jim Rankin returned to the Korean Peninsula. On May 24, 1952, they were given the incredibly difficult assignment at the Koje-do Island Prison Camp to restore operational control at this increasingly volatile Prison Camp.

They were not sent there to be prison guards. Instead they were charged with the responsibility of identifying the problem and proposing a solution. What they discovered almost immediately was that most of the POWs lived below ground and the camp was honeycombed with tunnels leading to other compounds.

They collected scores of barbed wire baseball bats and homemade zip guns, thousands of dollars of currency, hundreds of knives and spears made in the workshops, a working telegraph and 1,000 Molotov cocktails to kill or maim United Nations troops.

The paratroopers also discovered, "In one isolated part of the compound, the bodies of more than 50 anti-communist POWs, secretly executed and thrown down compound wells." They found the bodies of 100 others in unmarked shallow graves and enemy plans for the mass breakout of all 70,000 POWs.

When Sgt. Rankin arrived at the prison camp he was welcomed by unruly prisoners who greeted him with obscenities, rocks, and human excrement. As he recalled, "We had fought them once, now we were going to fight them again." At Koje-Do there was dirt everywhere. There were no concrete roads but dirt trails that ran between each compound.

It was a giant city of barber wire, huts and tents. There were still pockets of anti-communist Koreans who had been constricted by the North Korean People's Army as they swept into South Korea in the summer of 1950.

Each compound had its own system of justice. There were many innocent South Koreans who were tried in "Kangaroo Courts." The highest-ranking North Korean prisoner of war, Colonel Lee Hak who was both cunning and ruthless, sanctioned these courts.

Convicted prisoners had cotton forced down their throats, they were hung from barbed wire fences and stomped to death. In the words of then

Sgt. Jim Rankin, "The communist prisoners would execute anti-communist prisoners and then burn the bodies. We could smell flesh burning just about every night. The bodies would be carried out in honey buckets the next morning."

There were also a number of bizarre practices that the UN had allowed within each prison compound. For instance, each compound had its own metal workshop. The POW's were given gasoline to start fires and the compound gates were left unlocked to allow prisoners to interact with each other. It was not surprising that no American or UN guard would dare to enter a compound at night where beatings and murders committed by POWs went unpunished.

According to historian, Allan R. Millett, "Korean prisoners of war stood in sullen ranks, disciplined, belligerent, ready for battle even though their only weapons were homemade spears, clubs and incendiary grenades."

Within a short period of time, the new 187th leadership under the command of Brig. General Hayden "Bull" Boatner, decided their mission was to breakup the huge overcrowded compounds into smaller controllable units. This meant they would have to build a series of new compounds with a holding capacity of no more than 500 prisoners each. Sgt. Rankin helped to oversee this important effort and their mission was successful.

For over a month, small riots at the prison were met with tear gas grenades, bayonets and rifle butts. Finally, on June 14, 1952, the 187th moved into the rebellious compounds and vicious hand-to-hand combat ensured. According to official UN reports, there were 141 POW casualties at the prison. Order at Koje-do was finally restored.

Due to his leadership role in encouraging riots, attacking American troops and capturing General Dodd, North Korean Colonel Lee Hak's actions were not overlooked. *Life Magazine* reported that, "Colonel Lee was dragged away by the seats of his pants to solitary confinement for the remainder of the war."

Sgt. Jim Rankin completed his three-month tour of duty at one of the most infamous prison camps. Despite being there for only a short period of time, what happened at Koje-do was seared in Jim Rankin's memory forever. He told me, "I always conducted myself as a human being and then a soldier toward the prisoners. During my time at the camp, I didn't witness any cruelty by American soldiers toward the North Korean or Chinese prisoners." Sgt. Rankin added that, "There was no shortage of cruelty exhibited daily by the POWs who seemed to place little value on human life."

At the completion of this terrible assignment, Sgt. Jim Rankin and his band of 187th airborne brothers fought additional battles. Not only did he face a battle-tested enemy but also he endured, 40 to 50 degree temperatures below zero up in the mountains.

Fighting in Korea is not for the faint of heart. Temperatures are extreme. They are controlled by a large Siberian pressure system, which in the winter results in cold, dry northwesterly winds.

Between December 1st and February 28th, the average daily high temperature is minus 10 degrees Celsius. There were 5,300 frostbit casualties during the Korean War. One survivor wrote, "Once upon a time Hell froze over. We were there."

Sgt. Jim Rankin spent two miserable winters in a place that looked like an alien planet. He got to experience first-hand how his food and water froze. How batteries in Jeeps, radios and trucks quickly ran down. He witnessed how medical supplies froze and rifles became inoperative. The cold was as lethal as any Communist insurgent and if you spent enough time outside it had the effect of lulling soldiers into an often-fatal stupor.

According to Army Sergeant Charlie Gebhardt of Chicago, Illinois, "My feet were balls of lead. My fingers were turning black. You can't imagine how cold it was." Jim Rankin can certainly imagine because he lived through this experience. I am sure he was an expert on finding ways to stay warm. In fact, he opined that, "Korea was the coldest and most miserable place on the planet."

Among the ways American troops tried to not lose ears, fingers and toes was to poor gasoline into empty 105 mm shell canisters or directly into the dirt. They would simply light the gasoline and the result was instant heat. If there was no gasoline available, they found the nearest running tank or truck and found a spot behind the exhaust pipes. Ammunition, batteries and grenades were stored within a soldier's uniform. They were carefully protected like pictures of their loved ones back in the states.

In the summer, it is oppressively hot, humid and wet. It was almost unbearable. One of the last battles of the Korean War was fought between June 10th and July 20, 1953. It happened at Kumsong. Despite successful peace negotiations, South Korean President Syngman Rhee refused to sign the armistice. He even went so far as to infuriate the Chinese and North Koreans by releasing 27,000 North Korean prisoners who refused repatriation. In response, the outraged Chinese leadership launched an offensive at Kumsong involving 240,000 troops.

Opposing the Communists were 187,000 combat troops under the command of General Mark W. Kelly who was sent to stop them. The 187th Combat Airborne including the 11th Airborne Division played an essential role in this battle. After more than a month of combat, the brutal fighting finally stopped. It was the last large-scale Chinese offensive of the war and casualties on both sides were significant. U.S. forces suffered the loss of 305 troops Killed-In-Action, 1,981 wounded in combat and 70 captured by the Chinese. By contrast, there were 21,578 Chinese killed or wounded in the battle.

In his after-action report, General Mark W. Clark commented, "There is no doubt in my mind that one of the principal reason, if not the only reason, for the Communist offensive was to give the ROK's a bloody nose." Due to the actions of President Rhee, 2,286 American troops were killed, wounded or permanently disabled. There was absolutely no good reason why this battle occurred.

On July 27, 1953, a cease-fire was declared throughout the Korean Peninsula. At that time, Sgt. Jim Rankin was in the Kumwah Valley near the 38th Parallel. According to Mr. Rankin, "Two days before the fighting was supposed to stop, the Communists opened a fierce artillery barrage on our position. It didn't stop until the day after the cease fire."

During his two years in Korea, there were few happy moments for Sgt. Jim Rankin. He missed his family; the weather was tormenting and the enemy was always lurking just around the next hill. His only real happy memories were the brief time he got to spend at United Services Organization (USO) events in Korea. The USO was founded by "social reformer" Mary Shotwell Ingraham on February 4, 1941. It is an American non-profit organization with the singular goal of providing entertainment to members of the United States Armed Forces.

Between 1941 and 1945, a remarkable 7,300 entertainers performed in 420,000 performances to lift the spirits of 130 million servicemen and servicewomen in Europe and the Pacific theatre. The goal of these shows was to create an atmosphere of being their "Home Away From Home." Entertainers were paid $50 dollars a day. This was the equivalent of what an Army Private First Class received.

During the Korean War, these ambassadors spread their good cheer at UN and American bases throughout South Korea. Among those who made the trip to the combat zone were Errol Flynn, Cary Grant, Bob Hope, Al Jolson, Piper Laurie, Debbie Reynolds, Mickey Rooney and Jane Russell. The undisputed king of USO's with 57 shows during Second World War, Korea and Vietnam was Bob Hope.

This British born American comedian once said, "Believe me when I say that laughter up at the front lines is a very precious thing --- precious to those grand guys who are giving and taking the awful business that goes on there." Sgt. Jim Rankin was able to attend several of these shows and even met the indefatigable Bob Hope. These were incredibly uplifting events because for just a few brief moments, American troops got to forget about the daily horrors of the Korean War.

For most Fauquier County residents living in the early 1950's, the Korean War was a faraway conflict. It has been called the "Forgotten War." In Fauquier County, it was also the ignored war. The local newspaper, *The Fauquier Democrat* had no foreign correspondents nor did they utilize the *Associated Press* or R*euters* wire services. It is also impossible to know how many residents had subscriptions to *The Washington Daily News, The Washington Post* and *Washington Times-Herald.*

As a result, *The Fauquier Democrat's* coverage of the war was to largely ignore what was happening on the Korean Peninsula. During the first month of the war, Fauquier County residents were provided a "War Summary" at the bottom of the newspaper's front page. As the conflict progressed its coverage was limited to draft and induction notices, a new federal law requiring doctors and dentist to register for the draft and updates on county residents who were captured, wounded or sadly killed in Korea.

There was also an occasional human-interest story. The owner of the newspaper, Hubert B. Phipps loved to entertain his readership. In January 1951, he printed a story about 21-year old Marine Sgt. Clyde Deale of New Baltimore, Fauquier County, Virginia. The Sergeant was home on leave to recover from the frostbitten hands and feet he obtained at the bloody withdrawal of the Chosen Reservoir in North Korea in December 1950.

According to Sgt. Deale, "The Chinese poured down on us. I saw one armored half-truck over-run with Chinese though our crew was firing four machine guns steadily. There just were too many of them." United States forces comprised of the 1st Marine Division suffered the loss of 1,029 men, 4,894 were declared missing and 4,582 were wounded.

In April and May of 1952, *The Fauquier Democrat* printed a six part account entitled, "What war is like in Korea; A Fauquier Sergeant's Story." The author of the extended piece was Sgt. George Marsh of Catlett, Virginia. He was the commander of a group of five armored tanks. Sgt. Marsh recalled, "I assigned each tank to a certain area of the mountain so as to be sure that the entire mountain would be covered with fire at the same time. Then on a signal, we all started firing at once. With 20 machine guns and five 76-mm cannons we laid down a field of fire that the devil himself would have been afraid to stick his head up in."

In May of 1953, *The Fauquier Democrat* began a new regular feature called, "With Fauquier Men and Women In the Armed Forces." In its May 28, 1952 edition, there is an excellent picture and caption of Sgt. James A. Rankin. It reads: "Son of Mr. and Mrs. Clay Rankin of Midland is serving with the 187th Airborne Division in Japan and Korea. Sgt. Rankin enlisted in the Army in January, 1951." For those with loved ones serving in Korea, these articles were appreciated and uplifting.

Finally, in its July 30, 1953 edition, a writer for *The Fauquier Democrat* wrote,

"Korean Truce Will Free Fauquier Prisoners." This was welcomed news for the parents and families of Corporal James N. Wright of Catlett, Private First Class Henry Payne of Warrenton and Private First Class Eugene Reid of Warrenton.

After the longest negotiated armistice in history, fighting stopped throughout the Korean Peninsula at 10:00 a.m. on July 27, 1953. It had taken 158 meetings spread over two years and 17 days for representatives of North Korea, the People's Republic of China, the United Nations and the United States to agree to end the bloodshed.

The major components of the Korean Peace Armistice were: arrange the release and repatriation of prisoners of war; establish the Military Armistice Commission; prevent both sides from entering areas under the control of the other; suspend all hostilities and withdraw all military forces and equipment from the 2-mile wide "Demilitarized Zone."

During the same evening the agreement was signed, President Dwight David Eisenhower addressed the nation. He told the American people that, "Soldiers and sailors and airmen of sixteen different countries have stood as partners beside us throughout these long and bitter months. We have won an armistice on a single battlefield not peace in the world. We may not relax our guard nor cease our quest."

With the signing of the Armistice Agreement, many U.S. troops had earned the 48 points necessary to rotate back to the United States. A soldier received points for service overseas, decorations received, battle campaigns and how many children they had. During the Korean War, four points were awarded for every month served in close combat, two points each month for rear-echelon duty in Korea and one point each month for duty elsewhere in the Far East. Since the federal government was in charge of keeping track of each soldier's points, you could count on a significant lag time in the rotation process.

In early 1953, Sgt. Jim Rankin and 500 of his 187th airborne brothers were finally on their way home. They were transported on the *U.S.S. General John Pope.* Their journey to California would last 19 days but it was a far different experience than their arrival two years earlier. This time the troops were anxious to get home to see their parents, siblings and loved ones. In *The Rakkasans, 187th, The Steel Berets,* the author wrote", "During their voyage, the ship's captain told Gen. Westmoreland that his ship had carried many troops but none with the discipline and appearance of the Rakkasans."

According to Jim Rankin, he will always remember Camp Chickamauga in Buppu, Japan, its famous hot springs and Monkey Mountain that were a short distance from camp. In his words, "it was bitterly cold and snowing on the mountain every day." He finally arrived back in the United States and his final assignment was as a platoon sergeant at Fort Meade, Maryland. He was honorably discharged from the United States Army on January 9, 1954.

For some Americans, especially those who fought, the armistice was a unsatisfying end to a war that was never officially declared one by the United States Congress. Despite lasting only 1,085 days, the Korean War was exceptionally bloody. Nearly 5 million people died. Of this grim total, there were 36,574 Americans who died on the battlefield, 103,284 who had been wounded and 4,714 who had been taken as prisoners of war.

The number of those Americans killed in the Korean Conflict would have been much higher without the introduction of Mobile Army Surgical Hospitals (MASH's) in 1950. There were seven MASH units in Korea. They were staffed by 14 doctors, 12 nurses, 2 Medical Service Corps Officers, 1 Warrant Officer and 93 enlisted personnel.

If a soldier was wounded in battle, they would be transported to a MASH unit by helicopter. If a soldier was alive when he arrived at a MASH unit, they had a 95 percent chance of survival. More than 20,000 soldiers were treated during the entire conflict.

The concept of a MASH unit was the brainchild of the world's famous cardiovascular surgeon Dr. Michael E. DeBakey of Houston, Texas. Most Americans became familiar with these hospitals during the award winning television series MASH. This show lasted from 1972 to 1983 and its last episode, *Goodbye, Farewell and Amen* is the most watched television show of all time.

In Fauquier County, ten residents made the ultimate sacrifice for their country during the Korean War period. Those brave American heroes whose names are forever memorialized on the Fauquier Veterans Memorial are: Wallace V. Butler, Algernon S. Clowe, Stanley Ray Dennis, Paul T. Embrey, Clyde O. Gordon, Samuel S. Hall, III, David L. Kemper, Alfred H. King, Tyson R. Long and Russell Sieder. The most famous of those killed was Samuel Spencer Hall, III. He was the only child of Fauquier County Sheriff Samuel Spencer Hall II and Pearl Hamilton Hall.

This sacred wall on Hospital Hill in Warrenton, Virginia was dedicated on November 11, 1993. James Alvin Rankin was one of the twelve citizen members who served on the Fauquier Veterans Memorial Committee. Chiseled into the granite wall are the words, "This memorial is dedicated to the sons and daughters of Fauquier County who served their country in the United States Armed Forces."

In the Commonwealth of Virginia, 882 Americans who served in the Army, Air Force, Marine Corps, Navy and the United States Coast Guard died during active duty service in Korea. On a nationwide basis, Virginia had the 11th highest death toll with the State of California have the highest with 2,611 killed in action.

Since the last shot was fired during the Korean War control over the Korean Peninsula has changed little during the past seven decades. North Korean is still controlled by the same family of fanatics who constantly rattle their war swords while starving their own population. In South Korea, you have a democratically elected government, a stable and prosperous economy and South Korea is a strong ally of the United States.

During the 50th Anniversary of the War in 2000, Jim Rankin reflected that, "People didn't pay much attention to the Korean War at home unless some one of their family was over there. It's the same now. We still have men over there and there are still skirmishes. But no one seems to know or care. It is an area that has not known peace, and it's only a matter of time before the North Koreans will try to move on the South Koreans again." As of June 2022, there are still over 7,500 American personnel unaccounted for on the Korean Peninsula.

In the United States, as of December 30, 2020, there were over one million living veterans of the Korean War. Of this total, 27,554 lived in the Commonwealth of Virginia. The average age of these heroes is now between the upper 80's and the lower 90's. Of those Americans soldiers who served during the Korean War, 30,359 Bronze Star Medals were awarded.

Sergeant James Alvin Rankin of Fauquier County received two Bronze Star Medals for meritorious service in a combat zone during the Korean War. He also received the Korean Service Medal with three campaign stars, the Jump Wings and Combat Infantry Badge, the Syngman Rhee Ribbon and the Japanese Occupation Medal.

James Alvin Rankin is a lifelong member and a past 16th District Commander for the American Legion Post 72. This post was established in October 1919. It was officially named, at that time, the John D. Sudduth American Legion Post to honor his sacrifice in World War I.

The American Legion had been established on March 15, 1919 in Paris, France. The distinguished list of its founding members includes Lieutenant Colonel William "Wild Bill" Donovan, Lieutenant Colonel Theodore Roosevelt, Jr., Colonel Henry Stimson and Medal of Honor recipient Sergeant Alvin York.

The Warrenton Post was charted on August 1, 1920 and its first Commander was William Gordon Bartenstein (1880-1972). During his leadership term, James Alvin Rankin was responsible for signing the papers to develop the current property where the Post is located today at 345 Legion Drive, Warrenton, Virginia.

He is also a life member of the Warrenton VFW Post 9835, the 11th Airborne Division Association and the National Rakkasans Association that represents those serving in the 187th Airborne. James Alvin Rankin is a war hero and an American patriot.

The authors of the excellent book, *The Rakkasans* provided one of the best descriptions of patriotism. They wrote: "From the men who have given their lives, from the experiences of each airborne combat soldier learn what patriotism is. Patriotism is more than emotion. Patriotism is not an easy thing; sometimes it takes all of that we have; even our lives. But patriotism is a duty, an honorable and glorious duty, we are patriotic not for power, or position, or promotion, or money, or medals, but for love."

It is now 70 years since the armistice was signed and shooting stopped on the Korean Peninsula. Upon reflection, Jim Rankin stated that. "My service in Korea taught me more about the greatness of the United States than any other experience in my life. Service to this country is noble. I never regret my decision to enlist and would do so again without hesitation."

Jim Rankin went on to say, "'I am convinced that I survived the war because of my mother's prayers. My mother (Naomi Rankin) was a deeply religious and wonderful person."

Alice, Beverly, Shirley, Jim,
Alvin, & Glenn Rankin

Pvt. Clay Rankin

Meetze Road Bridge Dedication

Jim Rankin & Father Clay Rankin

Jim Rankin & Mother Naomi Rankin

The Class Picture

Photo courtesy of Eleanor Grohs Sumner

THE SIXTH GRADE at Bealeton High School in 1946. From left, front row, Dot Funkhouser, Bea Kane, Betty Cunningham, Mary Kemper, Leona Stribling, June Myers, Clara Cooper, Judy Chambers, Eleanor Grohs, Mary Bark; second row, Cletus Whitmer, Miss MacWelch, Betty Humberger, Sara Miller, Mary Encia, Earl Jacobs, Paul Cabbage, Archie Mason; back row, John Graves, James Rankin, Robert Hume, Thomas Rankin, McKinley Cunningham, Billy Embrey, Alvin Smith, Miss Mary Walter, teacher.

The Class Photo

John, Louise, Shirley & Jim Rankin –
Wedding Day

Fauquier County Supervisors: David Botts, James Rankin, Edwin Trenis, Jr., & Thomas Thorpe

The Rakkasan Reunion

Alvin & Juanita Rankin & Family

Jim Rankin & Alvin Rankin

Alvin, Glenn, & Jim Rankin

Kevin Rankin (Glenn's son)

Beverly & Loyd Alspaugh & Family

U.S. Amry Warrant Officer 3 Todd Alspaugh

Alice & Mike Kniceley

Harry, Jessica, Danny, Thomas, &
Lucas Bradshaw

Clara, Michelle, Owen & Bryan Kniceley

Kevin Rankin's Daughter Jessica &
Granddaughter Abby

American Legion Commanders Jim Rankin &
Roland Tapscott

Alice, Alvin, Jim, Glenn & Beverly

PFC Clay Rankin Memorial Bridge – Charles
Rankin, Jay Pinsky, Jim Rankin, Clay Rankin, III &
Lee Sherbeyn

Master Sgt. James Rankin

50th Anniversary of Rankin's

Kenny & Linda Rankin

Ann & Jesse Jenkins

The Rankin Family

128

Chapter 5: Humble Public Servant

Our third President, Thomas Jefferson, once wisely stated, "The care of human life and happiness is the first and only object of good government."

Since 1870, a five-member Board of Supervisors has governed the citizens of Fauquier County. The first Chairman was Gurley R. Hatcher of the Scott District.

There are five Magisterial Districts in Fauquier County. They are Cedar Run, Center, Lee, Marshall and Scott. Each member of the Board is elected for a four-year term and there are no limits on the number of terms or age for those who wish to serve.

According to its website, "The Fauquier County Board of Supervisors establishes priorities for county programs and services; establishes county legislative and administrative policies; appoints the county administrator and county attorney; adopts the annual budget; appropriates funds and sets the county tax rates." In 1983, the salary of a member of the Fauquier County Board of

Supervisors was about $10,000. Despite spending a considerable amount of time representing their constituents, most Supervisors have other full-time jobs.

On September 20, 1983, Robert James Keneflick who had represented the Center District on the Board of Supervisors resigned. This action became necessary because he no longer lived within the county. His new legal residency was in Culpeper. James F. Austin, who had previously served on the board from 1960 to 1976, was appointed to complete his unexpired term. Supervisor Austin chose not to run for re-election in November of 1983.

Prior to these developments, Jim Rankin declared on May 10, 1983 his candidacy for the Center District seat on the Board of Supervisors. In his announcement, Jim Rankin said, "I decided to run because I feel there is a need for someone who is familiar with the people and businesses in the county. Fauquier County has been good to me and I hope to make some measure of repayment as a member of the Board of Supervisors." Unlike many who run for political office, Jim Rankin wasn't interested in fame, power or glory. His singular goal was to improve the lives of his constituents in Fauquier County.

In 1983, every Constitutional Officer and member of the Board of Supervisors, except for one, was a member of the Democratic Party. As a lifelong small businessman who sold products to all consumers and someone who was only going to be beholden to his constituents, Jim Rankin choose to run as an Independent.

During the campaign, Jim Rankin promised the people of the Center District that he would support and work for a number of quality of life issues. These included: improving the public school system; proper land use planning; affordable housing for low income people; better recreational opportunities for all citizens; improved and expanded water and sewer services; an equitable tax structure and equal opportunities for all Fauquier County residents.

On the key issue of growth, Jim Rankin articulated his vision. He opined,

"They (Growth Pressures) should be accommodated to the rural nature of our county and at the same time not compromising working agriculture and other designated open space." As a small businessman, Jim Rankin believed in smart growth, while retaining the rural nature of Fauquier County. He rejected the idea that all commercial and residential development must be stopped.

In terms of education, Jim Rankin was a champion of the public school system. Each of his four children, Alvin, Glenn, Beverly and Alice, attended public schools in the county and graduated from Fauquier High School. In 1983, he stated, "Recruitment, retention and adequate pay for teachers are the most pressing problems in the county's public school system." As a result of his positions, Jim Rankin was one of only four candidates in the county to receive the endorsement of the Fauquier Education Association." In their press release, the Association noted, "These candidates are as concerned about your child's education as we are. Please remember them on November 8."

His opponent was Walter A. Hitchcock, Jr. who declared he too would file to run as an Independent candidate. Hitchcock was a West Point graduate, Korean War veteran and the President of the Warrenton Management Associates. He had also created a program called Jobshop that provided training to long term unemployed individuals.

Prior to the election, there were two troubling developments for Jim Rankin. The first was when former Board Member and now Culpeper resident, Robert J. Keneflick endorsed Walter Hitchcock. And, five days before voting, *The Fauquier Democrat* published a poll indicating 60 percent of Center District residents were planning to support Walter Hitchcock, 30 percent were voting for Jim Rankin and 10 percent were undecided. As someone who has worked on political campaigns, this is not the kind of news any candidate wants to hear especially right before Election Day.

On Tuesday, November 8, 1983, 65 percent of the 3,327 registered voters in the Center District cast their ballots for Supervisor. When the ballots were all counted, James Alvin Rankin had 1,183 votes or 52 percent and Walter Hitchcock had 1,0476 or 48 percent of the total vote. Despite the badly flawed pre-election poll and being outspent, Jim Rankin was elected the Center District Supervisor.

One week after the election, Jim Rankin wrote in *The Fauquier Democrat*, "I wish it was possible to thank personally, all who voted for and supported me for Supervisor --- and express to each of you, as I do here, my deepest gratitude and appreciation for your support. I shall do my best to justify your confidence in me."

Being a member of the Fauquier County Board of Supervisors is an arduous, tedious and time-consuming job. To be an effective member, Supervisors must not only attend Board meets but numerous public events, forums and public hearings. They must be available and responsive to the wishes of their constituents. It is a full-time job at part-time pay.

During 1983, there were 19 board meetings. Jim Rankin was present for every one. There were also various public hearings and site visits for new Supervisor Jim Rankin. This required hours of analysis, study and interaction with fellow board members. While most agenda items were approved by consent or unanimous vote, there were complex, expensive and contentious matters that came before the board. These required public hearings and the preparation of Resolutions to be voted upon by the five board members.

During Jim Rankin's initial eight years, a typical board meeting involved agreeing to the minutes of the prior get-together, presentation of the agenda and then discussing a number of miscellaneous items that could include: amendments to zoning ordinances, appointments to various entities, final plats, land use issues, quick claim deeds, recognitions, reduction of bonds, rezoning requests, right-of-way waivers, site plans, special exemptions and county tax rates.

The most important issue facing the board each year was the review and approval of the county's annual budget. At each meeting, time was always allocated for citizen and board members comments.

During his first term, Supervisor Rankin demonstrated outstanding leadership on a number of critical issues important to Fauquier County residents. These included: re-establishing the Library Trust Fund; the final plat and VDOT management for the Terranova Subdivision in Warrenton; tax exempt status for the Fauquier Hospital; Cable TV ordinance and negotiations with Prestige Cable of Warrenton; authorize issuance and sale of $500,000 general obligation school bond; deny efforts to dispose solid waste from Rappahannock County in a Fauquier County landfill; authorize $1.5 million to improve Fauquier High School's cafeteria and he led the effort to authorize the E-911 system in the county.

The most contentious issue of Jim Rankin's first term was a $30 million proposed school bond issue that had been approved by the Board of Supervisors. It was then submitted to Fauquier County voters. On March 5, 1987, Supervisors Sam Butler and Jim Rankin wrote in *The*

Fauquier Democrat, "We support the upcoming bond referendum because it gets our school building program off the ground. We urge all Fauquier citizens to register and vote YES! For the school bonds on Tuesday, March 31, 1987." Supervisor Rankin predicted, "I don't have any doubt about Center District supporting it."

The goal of the bond referendum was to develop plans for a new high school in the southern end of Fauquier County, a new elementary school in New Baltimore and badly needed improvements to other public schools in the county. This was a vital effort to improve educational opportunities for all Fauquier County public school students.

The leading opponents of the bond were the publisher of *The Fauquier Democrat* and a newly formed group called Committee for Fiscal Responsibility in Education. The membership of this group was largely made up of wealthy county residents who likely sent their children to private schools. They spent thousands of dollars to defeat the referendum proposal. They even ran a half-page advertisement in *The Fauquier Democrat* with the specious assertion that, "Your taxes will increase 42 percent." Their shortsighted argument was if you build new schools, people will move to Fauquier County.

On March 31, 1987, there were 17,367 registered voters in Fauquier County. On that fateful day, the school bond was defeated by a vote of 3,096 to 2,645. As predicted, Jim Rankin's Center District voted in favor of the referendum. The opponents had only managed to delay the construction of these two schools that would be built years later at a much higher cost.

Based on his impressive list of accomplishments, Jim Rankin decided to seek a second term on the Board of Supervisors. One of his constituents, Arthur C. Holland wrote, "Mr. Rankin is a very sincere and honest man of the highest integrity who wants very much to serve those constituents who elected him. I feel that he goes beyond what would be expected of an elected official. He deserves to be re-elected to the office he now holds."

In an April 23, 1987 interview with *The Fauquier Democrat,* Jim Rankin opined, "People come to me, I work on the problems and I try to resolve them. I have been available and people realize that." He went on to say, "Center residents want better schools, improved roads and more extensive services, such as water and sewer capacity." As he did for all his campaigns, Jim Rankin liked to get out and meet people in the community.

One Center District resident, now Captain Mark Jones of the Fauquier County Sheriff's Office remembers, "Jim Rankin used to ride through the neighborhood in his blue Lincoln and stop to ask folks for their vote and would they be willing to put up a campaign sign." Supervisor Rankin was always, "Confident the people will re-elect me in the fall."

His opponent in 1987 was Gary W. Watson who was born in Ponca City, Oklahoma, educated at Oklahoma University and owned a small business in Leesburg, Virginia. He had moved to Fauquier County in 1979. Watson's decision to run was somewhat shocking. Just a few months earlier on April 23,

1987, he told *The Fauquier Democrat,* "He's less interested in being a Supervisor than a few months ago." He added, "His Leesburg based printing business will require much of his attention."

During the campaign both candidates responded to a questionnaire provided by *The Fauquier Democrat* and they participated in a candidate forum on October 13, 1987. While each of them had supported the $30 million school bond, Gary Watson was opposed to enlarging service districts, expansion of water and sewer capacity, a state lobbyist for the county and an economic development officer. According to *The Fauquier Democrat,* James A. Rankin and Gary W. Watson couldn't be further apart in their beliefs on the major campaign issue of 1987 --- growth."

Supervisor Rankin noted, "The County must increase the building density for service districts to create more affordable housing for county residents." Unlike his opponent, Jim Rankin opposed the downzoning of farmland that would have changed the maximum of one home per five acres to a maximum of one home per ten acres." Supervisor Rankin passionately believes that property owners and not government should decide how to manage their land. His campaign slogan was, "James A. Rankin: Concerned Citizen. Working Supervisor."

As a relatively new county resident, Gary Watson views on development were virtually identical to those supported by the two most prominent anti-growth forces in the county. These organizations: Citizens for Fauquier County and the Piedmont Environmental Council are proudly responsible for killing Disney America in Prince William County, the Auburn Dam project, and many subdivisions in the county that were either delayed or stopped. In 1987, these groups endorsed Gary W. Watson.

By contrast, Jim Rankin, who had spent most of his 56-years living and owning a small business in Fauquier County that provided well paying jobs to county residents, had never forgotten his rural roots. He told *The Fauquier Democrat,* "He favors open spaces for subdivisions outside the service districts because we need to save our farms."

Despite these endorsements of Gary Watson, Jim Rankin was confident he would prevail on November 3, 1987.

When all the ballots had been counted, it was a photo finish between the two independent candidates. Jim Rankin had carried the Warrenton precinct by a vote of 735 to 516. This was a difference of 219 votes. At the same time, he lost the Baldwin Ridge precinct by a vote of 612 to 821. This was a difference of 209 votes. He had been re-elected Supervisor by a margin of ten votes. As a member of the Baldwin Ridge precinct since 1985, my wife and I were proud to have cast our votes for the Honorable James Alvin Rankin. A few friends in the county started to affectionately call him, "Landslide Rankin."

During his second term from 1988 to 1991, Supervisor Rankin took a leadership role in a number of key policy decisions. The two most important were the annual county budget and a new $18 million school bond. Each year, the Board of Supervisors receives a comprehensive budget proposal from the County Administrator. During this period, Steve

Crosby and G. Robert Lee served in that important position. Their recommendations were the product of hundreds of hours of analysis, careful calculations and tireless staff work.

The next step is a series of working sessions and then a public hearing allowing citizens to support or oppose any budget item. After this process is completed, the board can make additions or deletions to each expenditure and then the members vote on the final product.

During his service, there were few things more important to Jim Rankin than the budget process. His fundamental goals were to keep county taxes low, encourage smart growth and properly fund vital programs like the Health Department, the Public Libraries, the Sheriff's Office, Parks and Recreation, Community and Economic Development and most importantly the Fauquier County Public School System.

The second major issue was the $18 million school bond issue. This time four years later, the funds were approved and allocated to construct additions to four elementary schools, build two new elementary schools, expand the Fauquier High School cafeteria and develop the blue prints for the new high school that would open in September of 1994 as Liberty High School.

Supervisor Rankin was also actively involved in the establishment of a new lobbying policy for the Board of Supervisors; the creation of inspection fees for amusement rides; an appropriation of $15,000 to the Veterans Memorial Committee; a Resolution strongly supporting the Fauquier Head Start Program; a Resolution honoring the death of Fauquier County Sheriff's Sergeant Charles "Chuck" Murray; and a Resolution Supporting Fauquier County Veterans of the Persian Gulf War. He also nominated Roland Tapscott as the Citizen of the Year.

Roland Irvin Tapscott was an extraordinary man. He was a member of the United States Marine Corps during World War II that first opened their doors to enlisted black recruits in June of 1942. He was honorably discharged as a Corporal. Upon returning from the war,

Roland Tapscott spent his career in the federal government in the transportation office at the Washington Navy Yard. In Warrenton, he was a founding member of the Fauquier Housing Corporation that provided badly needed homes for low-income families.

He was a Past Commander of both the John D. Sudduth American Legion Post 72 and the Lt. Charles R. Anderson American Legion Post 360 in Warrenton, Virginia. After his death at the age of 91, Jim Rankin commented, "He was one of the best. He was like a brother to me. I really miss him." They had celebrated countless Memorial and Veterans Day parades, veterans' funerals and prayer breakfasts together.

On May 9, 1991, *The Times Democrat* ran a story entitled, "Rankin won't seek Center Board seat." In the article, Supervisor Rankin stated, "I said to start with that I was only interested in running for two terms. I think my business needs my support more than it has in the past."

Just prior to the Christmas holidays, Supervisors Jim Rankin and Wilbur Heflin were toasted by their colleagues at the County Courthouse. About 60 people were able to witness Board Chairman Jim Green present Jim Rankin with an uncooked chicken. His response was, "OH NO, OH NO, No Chicken for me." Rankin also received a lovely crystal bowl that was the perfect vessel for his rare fowl.

In the fall election, voters chose James G. Brumfield as their new Center District representative on the Board of Supervisors. At his first meeting on January 7, 1992, Brumfield submitted a Resolution that was unanimously adopted to commend the services of James A. Rankin as a member of the Board of Supervisors.

The Resolution read: "Whereas the services of Jim Rankin were characterized by an intense manifestation of conscientiousness and dedication to the causes of the common man as he was accessible to all and consistently took a leadership role in improving the standards of living and furthermore the quality of life for all citizens."

His successor, James Brumfield had dedicated his life to public service. He had moved to Fauquier County to become the Pastor of the Marshall United Methodist Church. Brumfield had also been an elementary school teacher in the county and retired after 30 years of service as Fauquier County's Deputy School Superintendent.

He served on the Board of Supervisors for six years until his untimely passing on December 7, 1997 at the age of 63. Today, one of the county's institutions of learning is named the James G. Brumfield Elementary School. This was a fitting tribute to a man who loved to teach young minds.

With his death, it became necessary to appoint someone to fill his Board seat until the November election in 1998. According to press reports, there were 19 candidates who applied for the position. They were carefully screened, vetted and debated by the remaining four board members. Without question, the board selected and approved the most qualified person for the Center District vacancy.

In the Resolution, it stated, "Resolved by the Board of Supervisors of Fauquier County this 23rd day of December 1997, That James A. Rankin, a qualified voter of Center Magisterial District be, and is hereby, appointed as the Interim Supervisor of the Center District Magisterial District until such time as a successor is elected and has qualified in conformance with state law."

When advised of the appointment, Jim Rankin responded, "I appreciate the offer and I accept it." It had been six years since he had served on the board. Nevertheless, based on his vast experience in business and local government, Jim Rankin knew how to write a county budget, keep taxes low and prioritize the most important county programs. He had also never lost his intense desire to help his constituents and to work to improve their lives.

Lifelong educator and Fauquier High School government teacher, Benjamin McCartney told *The Times Democrat,* "I wouldn't have any problem with him (Rankin). He tends to be the most like Jim Brumfield. I would have a major problem if we went unrepresented. Anyone unfamiliar with the financial process is going to be behind the eight ball coming in."

On January 6, 1998, Jim Rankin attended his first meeting as the new Interim Supervisor. He joined a board that had: Chairman David C. Mangum, Vice Chairman Larry L. Weeks, Wilbur W. Burton and James R. Green, Jr. He was given assignments on the Joint Dispatch Center Board of Directors, Personnel Committee, Public Safety Committee, Radio Study Committee and Team Tourism.

One of his first decisions was to name Charles E. Hall, Jr. as the Center District Citizen of the Year. Hall was an architect who served with distinction for many years as the Center District representative on the Fauquier County Planning Commission.

During the 1998 term, there were a number of highly controversial matters before the Board of Supervisors. These included a three-cent increase in the county real estate tax, the proposed construction of the Auburn Dam, the Waterfield Subdivision and the Route 28 four-lane widening project. Each of these had been supported by a majority of the Board of Supervisors.

The modest revenue increase unanimously approved by the Board of Supervisors raised the real estate tax from $1.03 to $1.06 of $100 of assessed value. It was necessary to close a $2 million revenue shortfall. It was painful decision for Jim Rankin. The shortfall had occurred before he rejoined the board. Nevertheless, in his words, "They had no other plausible choice. It was dumped on my lap." This was the first time in five years, Fauquier County residents would have to pay more in real estate taxes that funded the county's public school system.

The idea of a new 183-acre reservoir to provide municipal drinking water to the New Baltimore area and flood control to southern Fauquier farmers was the brainchild of the U.S. Department of Agriculture. There were seven watershed projects designed to improve flood mitigation around Virginia. Six had already been built by 1998. After extensive deliberations and public hearings on the proposal, the Board of Supervisors approved its construction.

Edwin F. Gulick, a member of the John Marshall Soil and Water Conservation District Board, penned a guest column in the October 29, 1998 edition of *The Fauquier Citizen.* According to board member Gulick, "The Auburn Dam project had enjoyed unanimous government approval for over 30 years including passage in the U.S. Congress." He went on to add, "Not only will this project be good for the future of Fauquier County, but it will be essential to the preservation of farming and agriculture to those farmers downstream who continually lose topsoil, infrastructure and livestock to the floods."

The Citizens for Fauquier County, the Piedmont Environmental Council and other no growth advocates argued that the dam would create a boom for commercial and residential development. Jim Rankin supported the Auburn Dam project. It was ultimately never built because of endless lawsuits filed by both national and local environmental organizations.

A third issue was the construction of the Waterfield Subdivision of 667 homes in the Vint Hill area. This project had been approved on a 3 to 2 vote. Supervisor Rankin stated, "Waterfield was a tough one. And I worked hard to get those numbers (houses) down from the 1,600 homes originally proposed two years earlier." The Waterfield developer had made a $4 million dollar proffer to expand the wastewater treatment plant at the Vint Hill Farms station.

Jim Rankin also noted, "Vint Hill's in the planning stage but without Waterfield, we have no money for sewer." While there is no Waterfield Subdivision within the county, the 667 homes were built and became part of the existing Brookside homes in the Scott Magisterial District.

Finally, the Board unanimously voted to widening Route 28 in Fauquier County. This highway then carried about 10,000 vehicles a day between Nokesville and Remington. Arabelle Arrington told

The Fauquier Citizen, I urge you to take into consideration the number of fatal accidents on this road." In the spring of 1996, seven people died on Route 28. Supervisor Larry Weeks noted, "As long as citizens have four service districts, we have no choice but to go ahead with four-lands on Route 28."

Despite the Board of Supervisors approval, this project was never undertaken. Once again, the no-growth advocates were instrumental in stopping it and thus denying improvements in highway safety for the tens of thousands of people who have used Route 28 in the past 25 years.

In a somewhat surprising move, Jim Rankin announced he would run to complete the final year of Jim Brumfield's term. His fellow Board Member Wilbur Burton stated, "Rankin has the experience necessary to do the job, is a successful businessman and a lifelong resident who knows the problems of the county. I endorse Jimmy Rankin."

On March 25, 1998, newcomer Joe Winkelmann of Taylor, Texas announced he would run for the Center seat as a Republican. Joe Winkelmann discovered Warrenton by accident. He and his wife Laurie were riding their Harley-Davidson to Charlottesville when they made a wrong turn and ended up on Main Street in Warrenton. In 1996, they found a house "For Sale" at 100 Culpeper Street and promptly purchased it. For the next two years, he wrote a weekly column for *The Times Democrat* known as "Telling Tales."

Who was Joe Winkelmann? He was born and raised in Williamson County, Texas. Graduated from Trinity College in San Antonio, Texas and arrived in Washington, D.C. as a staffer for Texas U.S. Senator John Tower in 1975. After a brief period of Capitol Hill service, Joe Winkelmann spent ten years as a lobbyist for the National Association of Realtors and served as the Chief of Staff for the Realtors Political Action Committee. The purpose of this job was to recommend the issuance of checks to members of Congress who supported the real estate industry.

After less than two years living in Fauquier County, Winkelmann decided to seek public office. While every American has a right to run for any elective office, Joe Winkelmann was a carpetbagger. He had never held public office, never been involved in public safety and never voted for a Fauquier County Constitutional Officer or a member of the Board of Supervisors. When he filed his candidacy, he knew virtually nothing about the Center District or the people who lived there.

My only interaction with him occurred on Father's Day in 1986. Between 1981 and 1995, I worked as the Legislative Director and then Committee Chief of Staff for Congressman Jack Fields of Humble, Texas. As a member of his staff, I was allowed to participate in activities sponsored by the Texas State Society. This group had functions throughout the year but the only one I and my family attended was the annual Father's Day Picnic. These were huge lavish parties with hundreds of guests, live Texas music, games and prizes and spectacular barbeque.

On June 15, 1986, the celebration was held at the J.R. Stockyards Festival Lakes in Leesburg, Virginia. As I did every year, I played bingo with about 200 to 300 guests. For the first and only time I won a game of bingo. The prize was an assortment of Texas products worth about $100.

Upon winning I was asked by the President of the Texas State Society to give my name and hometown. I proudly announced my name and my residence in Warrenton, Virginia. Hearing that news, the President encouraged the Texas audience to greet me with a loud round of boos. My tormentor that day was Texas State Society President Joseph "Joe" Winkelmann of Washington, D.C.

Upon hearing of his desire to run for Center District Supervisor, one county resident, John Kendrick, wrote *The Times Democrat* in the fall of 1998. He asked, "Who is this guy, Joe Winkelmann? I believe one of the most important qualifications of a Supervisor is organization and the ability to finish what he starts. The only thing I can see Winkelmann has accomplished around here is to totally plaster the town with his pretty blue campaign posters."

The election of November 3, 1998 was nasty. Jim Rankin ran on his outstanding record. He reminded the people of Center District that, "I've always served the people in my District with their interests in mind. I'm an independent voice on the Board of Supervisors." On the key issue of education, a paid political advertisement noted, "Education. Parents and Children can trust Jim Rankin when it comes to support our public schools. Can we trust his opponent? No! He promised the teachers that he's on their side but he wants to slash support to the schools by 10%."

Civil Rights icon and Fauquier County School Board member, John E. Williams wrote, "A 10% cut to the schools budget may mean losing 132 teachers. This would affect about 4,000 students and art, music and physical education programs. It just doesn't make sense! That's why I support Jim Rankin, a proven friend of our public schools!"

In a full-page article in the fall of 1998 in *The Times Democrat*, Jim Rankin outlined his vision for the future, "I want to see Fauquier County with a solid public school system, abundant and clean drinking water and sanitation systems, safe roads, profitable exploitation of the former Army base at Vint Hill and a sensible policy of bringing quality commercial and industrial development to Fauquier County."

On October 8, 1998, there was a candidate forum at the First Baptist Church Family Life Center in Warrenton. It was a two-hour debate with about two hundred interested potential voters in the audience. Despite being a paid real estate lobbyist, Joe Winkelmann embraced the no growth agenda of The Citizens of Fauquier County and the Piedmont Environmental Council. During the debate, Winkelmann indicated he strongly opposed the Auburn Dam, expansion of Route 28, Waterfield housing project and the recently approved tax increase.

Winkelmann advised the voters of the Center District that, "There is no need for Auburn Dam. From a flood control standpoint, it would be far cheaper for the county to buy all of the land from every farmer down stream that ever gets flooded and turn it into a park."

Unfortunately, what he failed to explain to the public was the proposed cost of these agricultural lands, whether eminent domain would be utilized and how much in taxes would be permanently lost to Fauquier County by converting farmland to parks.

During the campaign, Republican Supervisor Larry Weeks placed a campaign advertisement in *The Times Democrat* stated, "Joe will be a strong ally in our efforts to keep taxes down." I find this interesting and hypocritical. Supervisor Weeks not only voted in favor of the 3-cent increase but it was his idea in the first place. It was Larry Weeks who correctly argued the increase was critical to retaining talent in our public school system.

Winkelmann even opposed extending public utilities to Wal-Mart. While Jim Rankin was concerned about the potential impact this huge store would have on local small businesses, he thought it was absurd to deny them utilities after the construction of the building. Candidate Winkelmann also promised to abolish the Center District Advisory Committee established by Jim Rankin. Despite never having attended a meeting of the Advisory Committee, his rationale was, "It has lost its way, serving a narrow agenda of the few people, rather than the broader, public good." How was allowing local citizens to have a greater voice in their local government was a bad idea? He failed to answer that important question.

In response to these positions, Jim Rankin said, "I would say he doesn't have the business experience. He hasn't lived here long enough to know the county. You have to know the lay of the land before you know whether its suitable or not." The choice for the residents of Center District was stark. Jim Rankin was a lifelong resident, highly successful small businessman, war hero and dedicated public servant. Joe Winkelmann was none of those things. He had just settled in

Warrenton and had just opened a travel agency with his wife.

During the 1998 campaign, Jim Rankin wanted to see smart growth at the former Vint Hill Military Base. His opponent unbelievably wanted to get rid of Vint Hill. Today, there are more than 2,000 well paying jobs within the revitalized Vint Hill base community. In his closing argument, Supervisor Jim Rankin reminded the citizens of the Center District that by voting for him, they would get: "No Smoke, No Mirrors. Just Good, Honest Government!" This is exactly what they had received from him for nearly nine years on the Board of Supervisors.

There were many Fauquier County residents who strongly supported Jim Rankin and his lifetime of service. Dr. Lewis Springer said, "Jim Rankin has my vote because he is the most qualified person for Center District supervisor." Fauquier Hospital nurse, Gwen Connor noted, "When I think of Jim Rankin I think of community service. I grew up in Fauquier and even as a child I remember him helping out with many organizations.

I wouldn't think of voting for anyone else this year."

Tamie Robinson, the Commissioner of Fauquier Youth Football wrote in 1998, "Jim Rankin is dedicated to making this county a better place. He's helped out with Fauquier Youth Football in many ways from giving us space for our equipment to helping with registration. He does whatever he can. His actions speak louder than words."

Tracy Damone opined, "I'm voting for Jim Rankin because I know how dedicated he is to seeing that the children of this county get the best possible education."

Kathryn A. Carter of Warrenton wrote, "I would like to express my gratitude to Jim Rankin for his service to the citizens of Center District, as well as to all of Fauquier County under the most trying of circumstances."

Virginia Craun noted, "He's a local man and a most generous man. He's from the county and he's given back to the county." And, Shirley Smoot said, "I vote for Mr. Rankin. I know what he has done for the community. I feel he is an honest man and I'm not against growth in this county."

Nevertheless, Joe Winkelmann had a number of political advantages in 1998. Since it was a special election, he shared the ballot with popular Republican Congressman Frank Wolf. In addition, Virginia Republican Governor Jim Gilmore, Republican Sheriff Joe Higgs, Warrenton Mayor George Fitch, the Fauquier Education Association, The Citizens of Fauquier County, the Piedmont Environmental Council and *The Times Democrat* endorsed Winkelmann.

In an ironic twist, there were a number of folks supporting Winkelmann who had recently moved to Fauquier County to find their little slice of heaven. Sadly, many of them thought it was appropriate to slam the door on anyone else who wished to live here.

With his DC lobbying connections, Winkelmann raised over $30,000 that he used to dominate the airwaves, flood the newspapers and place hundreds of yard signs through Center District. His financial haul from both real estate and no growth advocates was three times as much as Supervisor Jim Rankin was able to collect.

On November 3, 1998, the voters of Center District went to the polls and elected an unknown man from Taylor, Texas as their new Supervisor. He would soon unveil his self-described vision as "The Ax Man" on the Board of Supervisors. Winkelmann's stated goal was to substantially cut the Fauquier County budget.

On the night of the election, Jim Rankin visited Winkelmann's Culpeper home to congratulate the Supervisor-Elect. He wished him well and offered, "If I can help you in any way, I'd be glad to." When asked by the local media his reaction to the election, Jim Rankin said, "I'm not crying over it. It may be a relief. Trying to run a business and putting in the time with the board isn't easy. This certainly will give me a break." When asked, Winkelmann praised Jim Rankin for his work on the board. He added, "Jim Rankin is a Warrior."

Warrenton resident, Rich Galecki, who served as Jim Rankin's campaign manager noted, "And despite the Fauquier Education Association's shocking endorsement of his opponent, Rankin will always be a friend to our teachers, administrators and school support personnel. The people in the Center District have just turned their backs on a good man and a dedicated Supervisor."

On December 1, 1998, the Board of Supervisors unanimously, including Joe Winkelmann, approved a Proclamation of Recognition and Commendation for James A. Rankin. It said, "Whereas during his interim term as a member of the Fauquier County Board of Supervisors, James A. Rankin continued his previous course of improving the standards of living and furthering the quality of life for all citizens of Fauquier County."

As a postscript, Joe Winkelmann was re-elected in 1999 but decided not to run for a second four-year term. He told *The Washington Post* that, "He is no longer essential to the future of Fauquier County." Winkelmann added that, "He hates the political game." During his five years as a Supervisor, he earned his nickname of "The Ax Man" by leading the charge to cut funding for popular programs like the County Library System, Parks and Recreation and the Sheriff's Office.

Despite endorsing Winkelmann, Sheriff Joe Higgs and his agency were not immune from budget reductions. In fiscal years 2003 and 2004, the Sheriff's Office received $772,921 less than it requested. After completing his term in 2003, the Winkelmann's sold their Culpeper house and travel agency and moved out of Fauquier County quicker than a Texas Tornado.

During his almost nine years on the Board of Supervisors, Jim Rankin had several fundamental principles. These were fairness, openness, honesty and integrity. While it is always more difficult to win an election as an independent candidate, Jim Rankin was steadfast in his belief that, "I can serve the interest of the entire District because I am not owned or influenced by special interest groups who so often want concessions for their own narrowly defined reasons."

During one of his first meetings as Supervisor, Jim Rankin met with a powerful conservation entity in the county. After exchanging pleasantries, the group told him they expected him to support a number of their priorities. After politely listening to their pitch, Jim Rankin said, "I am here to support my constituents. If our views align that would be fine. If they don't, I will be voting with the people." This group never forgave him for his honesty.

In many ways, Jim Rankin was the pivotal third vote on the Board of Supervisors. While he never wanted Fauquier County to become Fairfax, Loudoun or Prince William, he understood that we should share the beauty and splendor of Fauquier with those young families who simply couldn't afford to live closer to the District of Columbia. There was also an absolute need to expand the county tax base to pay for vital services.

During his nine years on the Board, Jim Rankin attended 206 out of 210 meetings. He had perfect attendance in 1984, 1985, 1986, 1987, 1990 and 1998. In his own words, "I spent over 48 hours a week on the job as Supervisor of Center District, in addition to my regular occupation making a living for my family. This is more than most people spend on their regular jobs. I also attended meetings of seven official committees to which I'm assigned. The sacrifice is worth it to make our quality of life better."

Jim Rankin made 69 appointments to various county authorities, boards, commissions, committees, councils and task forces. The most appointments were for the Building Appeals Board, Parks and Recreation, Agriculture and Forrestal District Advisory Committee, Industrial Development Board, Water and Sanitation Authority and the County Planning Commission. According to the former Supervisor, his best appointment was to name Roland Tapscott to two consecutive four-year terms on the County Planning Commission. Mr. Tapscott was the first African American appointed to a major Fauquier County position.

As President John Fitzgerald Kennedy famously stated in his 1961 Inaugural Address to the nation, "Ask not what your country can do for you ... ask what you can do for your country." Jim Rankin lives that aspiration every day. He has never had any regrets about his public service. One of his greatest achievement was to represent his constituents living in the Center District. This is how representative government should work as articulated by our founding fathers.

Fauquier County is a better place because of the caring, effective and tireless leadership of James Alvin Rankin on the Fauquier County Board of Supervisors.

Chapter 6: Customer Service

In the 19th Century, American author Horatio Alger, Jr. of Chelsea, Massachusetts, wrote nearly 100 books for young adults. His persistent theme was to highlight teenage boys who experienced a "Rags to Riches" life.

These boys, who were born into poverty, worked to earn money for their families' survival as clerks, detectives, farmhands, messengers, miners and newsboys. In every book, they overcame adversity and achieved success because of their courage, determination, hard work, honesty and perseverance.

James Alvin "Jimmy" Rankin could have been a real life character in one of Horatio Alger's novels. Since taking his first steps, Jim Rankin has worked at a variety of jobs. His first experiences were working on the family farms in Fauquier County. This required countless hours of planting, cultivating, feeding, weeding and helping to harvest the crops that fed his entire family during the Great Depression.

Before enlisting in the United States Army, Jim Rankin worked as a carpenter's helper, grocery clerk at the Vint Hill Farms Station Commissary, the A&P grocery store on the Quantico Marine Base and was employed at the Trenis General Store in Catlett, Virginia.

After his heroic service on the Korean Peninsula, he resumed his life in Fauquier County. One of his jobs was as a laborer and truck driver for the now defunct Sanders Quarry in Calverton, Virginia. Jim Rankin also restarted his employment at the Trenis' Store.

The Trenis family had operated a series of small businesses in Fauquier County since 1866. Bertrand E. Trenis opened his first General Store on Elk Run Road in Catlett one year after the end of the American Civil War. During the next 153 years, generations of Trenis' successfully operated convenience stores, gas and propane stations, hardware stores and a Trenis IGA grocery store with some of the best-fried chicken. At one point, they even sold dynamite, Ford cars and Minneapolis Moline tractors.

Jim Rankin was a dedicated, hard working and loyal employee. Due to his superb work ethic, he was named the manager of the new Trenis Gas and Appliance Store in Warrenton, Virginia. This business opened on July 15, 1960 and was incorporated within its General Store in Catlett five years later. During its brief Warrenton tenure, Trenis' sold custom built kitchens, Tappan gas stoves and Phillips 66 Philgas. The family motto in Catlett was, "It's a little out of the way, but a lot less to pay."

For many years, the Trenis family would host a summer picnic for family and employees. On August 3, 1955, one of those gatherings was celebrated at the Fairview Beach in King George County, Virginia. Jim Rankin remembers attending several of those picnics and the importance of treating employees with kindness. Edwin M. Trenis firmly believed that, "If you want to keep your customers happy, start by keeping your employees happy." Jim Rankin certainly believes in this philosophy.

It was about this time that the owner of what is now the Warrenton

Village Center, Aaron Gerber of the District Properties of Washington and Robert Gilliam, who managed the shopping center, urged Jim Rankin to open his own hardware store.

Robert Lawrence Gilliam was a combat pilot and flight instructor during both World War II and the Korean Conflict. He retired as an Air Force Captain receiving both the Distinguished Flying Cross and Purple Heart. He managed both the Northern Virginia Shopping Center and the Warrenton Village Shopping Center from 1960 to 1994. During this period, Bob Gilliam served on the Fauquier County Board of Supervisors representing the Center District and Chairman of the County Board of Education.

Jim Rankin's initial response to their suggestion was, "I had no money. I had a wife, four little children and I was 35 years old. So I hocked my house. We were living in a little brick house I built at St. Stephen's in Catlett, Virginia." He told the local press, "I wasn't nervous at all about starting my own business. I have always had confidence in myself, however, my wife was a little nervous. We were a young family to be mortgaging the house."

With a $22,000 investment, Jim Rankin rented the 4,500 square foot building from Aaron Gerber. Prior to the hardware story's opening 10-year old Alvin and 8-year-old Glenn Rankin were already working with their dad to fix up the store, stock the shelves and get it ready to be open to the public.

Jim Rankin's initial paid employees included Steve Hanback, Joe Heddings, Randy Moore, Danny Payne and Vinton Williams. Danny Payne was the first manager. The "Grand Opening" of the new Rankin's True Value Hardware was Friday, March 18, 1966.

On that day, customers could buy a brand new Zenith "25" rectangular color TV for $219. They also received 10 percent off "all hardware items, farm and garden tools and supplies." The tag line was: "Shop and Save in our Big Grand Opening Specials!"

Throughout American history, small businesses, like Rankin's Hardware, have been the economic backbone and engine of this great country. One of our nation's most well known entrepreneurs started out as a small businessman. His name was Sam Walton of Kingfisher, Oklahoma. With just a few dollars, he started a business empire that today includes 10,623 Wal-Mart's throughout the world and 600 Sam's Club stores. His advice to other small businesses was, "The goal as a company is to have customer service that is not just the best but legendary."

Jim Rankin has always been a shrewd businessman. After opening Rankin's True Value Hardware, he understood he would have to compete with Blue Ridge Hardware, Risden Paint and Hardware and Warrenton Supply. These entities were all located in the same Warrenton community.

Jim Rankin's motto, since the first day he opened the doors, has been, "Quality products, outstanding customer service, great prices and caring about the people who live in the community." He also made it clear to each new employee that they were more than just workers but family members.

This strategy of treating your employees with respect and as extended members of the Rankin family has paid huge dividends in terms of loyalty. Since opening, Rankin's Hardware had a number of employees who had worked for him for over 20 years. The list includes Barbara Edwards, Sandra Jeffries, Mike Kniceley and Ann Jenkins who, as of this writing, have been working at Rankin's Hardware and Rankin's Furniture for 53 years as the primary bookkeeper. According to Jim Rankin, "Ann Jenkins has been my right hand person for over five decades."

In those early days of 1966, Jim Rankin did something ingenious. In his words, "I would buy two or three of each item, wait until I sold it, then purchase a few more the next time, slowly building up on my inventory" During this period, Rankin's Hardware was growing about 25 percent each year.

Unfortunately, the store was small and the opportunity to expand to other lines of products was restricted. Jim Rankin remembers, "It seemed like just one big store. We had it packed full. For a while there was only a path to get across the place." In a good way, they had outgrown the original Rankin's Hardware.

In February of 1973, his next-door neighbor at 681 Northern Virginia Shopping Center, the Easton's Menswear and Shoes Store, caught fire. According to one of the Easton's employees, Frank Ramey, "I will never forget how much work it was to clean up a total loss of that store. I do remember that there was a gentleman from the Food Lion that supposedly saw the bulging of the front window from the heat, and he threw something through it. Once the air hit the front of that store, it was fully engulfed and a total loss."

This fire not only badly damaged James Easton's store but caused a great deal of soot and smoke damage to Rankin's Hardware. Ironically, for the two months prior to the fire, Easton's ran a weekly ad in *The Fauquier Democrat* proclaiming that the "store was closing," "going out of business" and "final days."

At the time of the blaze, the Rankin's were enjoying one of their rare family vacations in Corpus Christi, Texas. They had to immediately drive back to Warrenton to deal with this catastrophe. In fact, they were forced to sell many of their damaged products at about 25 percent of their original value. Mr. James Easton opted not to re-open his Menswear and Shoe store.

Instead, Jim Rankin decided to rent the Easton space after the fire damage restoration process was completed. It had always been his goal to have every product that a potential customer might need. With this new expansion, this section of the Rankin store became the showroom for new Zenith television sets and furniture to enjoy NFL football games.

On March 14, 1973, Jim's younger brother, Charles "Charlie" Rankin signed a contract for a new Rankin's Menswear and Shoes in the Warrenton Village Center. It was conveniently located just next door to the other two Rankin stores. In this well stocked haberdashery, they sold the top brands of clothing such as Cricketeer suits and Harris Tweed jackets, Munsingwear polo shirts, Van Heusen dress shirts and Florsheim shoes.

On January 19, 1978, a customer could purchase from Charlie Rankin, his son Lawrence or Frank Ramey, a pair of outstanding Florsheim footwear for $29.95. The store also had available for rent, tuxedoes for special occasions like dances and weddings. All of these products, except Harris Tweed of Scotland, were manufactured in the United States.

In the winter of 1978, Rankin's True Value moved to the current location of the hardware store. This additional space immediately expanded the True Value Hardware to 20,000 square feet. With this significant increase in floor space, it wasn't long before the store started to stock appliances, building materials, lawn mowers, snow blowers, television sets and video equipment.

The store also offered to repair appliances and they had the ability to make hundreds of keys to satisfy the customer's needs. There are few things in life more frustrating than losing an important key or breaking one off in your front door. Jim Rankin and his fine staff were always ready to alleviate your crisis by making a replacement key at a reasonable price.

Jim Rankin had the idea of creating specific self-sustaining departments. This was about the same time VHS tapes became the rage throughout the United States. Rankin's was the second business in Warrenton to rent BETA and VHS videos. They also sold the large cumbersome VHS players, offered to fix these machines and rented tapes for a one-time subscription fee.

A second department was the sporting goods section. In the 1980's, there were no Dick's Sporting Goods, Modell's or Wal-Marts located in Fauquier County. If you needed new sports attire or gear, Rankin's Hardware was your one-stop designation. It had or could order anything a sports enthusiast would need for their favorite pastime.

A third department was the actual hardware store. It was here where professional carpenters, electricians and plumbers came to obtain the necessary items they needed to properly service their customers. This was long before you could simply order products on your cell phone and have them expeditiously delivered by Amazon. There were no BJ Warehouses, Costco's or Sam's Clubs. It was also a great place for homeowners to obtain suggestions on how to "Do-It-Yourself" projects.

When the Rankin's Menswear and Shoes store closed, it became Rankin's Sporting Goods. Mike Kniceley and Charlie Rankin successfully managed it. It offered a cornucopia of sporting equipment for every season as well as dress shirts and sports footwear. Five years later, the store was moved to the Rankin's Waterloo Shopping Center. In 1999, it was incorporated within the Rankin's Hardware Store.

In 1992, there were 38 employees working at the Rankin's Hardware Stores in Colonial Beach and Warrenton. At the flagship store in Warrenton, son Alvin Rankin was the General Manager, daughter Alice Rankin Kniceley was the inventory manager, brother Charles Rankin and son-in-law Mike Kniceley were in charge of sports goods and nephew Kent Rankin was the man to see in the hardware section. Daughter Beverly Rankin Alspaugh and her husband Loyd and Glenn Rankin were doing an outstanding job managing the successful Rankin's True Value Hardware Stores in Colonial Beach and Winchester, Virginia.

During this same year, I was the Registrar of the Fauquier County Babe Ruth Baseball League. My two sons, Rick and Chris, were playing on one of the teams that I coached with John Fossard, Kevin Kelly, Ed Warmus and the late Allan Dotson.

Every year before the season started in March, I would meet with other age appropriate coaches in Jim Rankin's office at the hardware store. Mike

Kniceley would conduct the annual draft where players were assigned to certain teams. This was always a well-organized process due to the outstanding efforts of Mike Kniceley.

Each coach was allocated with balls, hats, stirrups, a coacher's mitt and uniforms for the season. While most uniforms were basic, Judge Dudley Payne would always outfit his players with real major league uniforms and hats. He coached the team along with the late Dr. Doug Clarke and real estate lawyer Tom Ross. There were some in the county who referred to his team as the "Million Dollar Boys Club."

Since all of the games were played at Fauquier County Public Schools, the preparation of the field was the responsibility of the coach who was the home team for that game. Rankin's always provided the dry lime dust and calcined clay necessary for the batters box, foul lines and pitcher's mound.

As a coach, I outfitted my own children with Rankin's batting gloves, cleats, extra baseballs, gloves and new expensive aluminum bats. While I grew up using wooden Louisville slugger bats by the late 1970's aluminum bats, first manufactured by the Worth Bat Company of Tullahoma, Tennessee in 1970, were being used extensively in Babe Ruth, colleges, high schools and Little League Baseball.

Over the years, my family would frequently visit Rankin's Hardware. In the spring, we would stop and purchase flower and vegetable seeds, tomato, squash and cucumber plants, geraniums, marigolds and pansies. We seem to buy endless amounts of birdseed. For the house, there was always a need for a box of nails or screws, caulk, gravel, paint supplies, plumbing items and yard equipment. I would procure bags of mulch to spread throughout my yard.

Over the course of more than 30 years, I purchased dozens of keys, bags of old fashion candy, fall mums and the annual White House Christmas Ornament. Since 1981, the White House Historical Association has been annually selling ornaments commemorating our U.S. Presidents.

Since 1985, I had been buying them from the Rankin's True Value Hardware. In 2023, the Historical Association will celebrate the life and Presidency of Gerald R. Ford, Jr. of Grand Rapids, Michigan.

I had the great honor to work on his Presidential campaign in 1976 and to watch fireworks celebrating our nation's 200th Anniversary of our Independence at the White House with Jimmy and then Candy Willis of Warrenton. I will never forget this outstanding display of American patriotism or the hideous baby blue leisure suit President Ford was wearing on the balcony of the White House.

A few months later, my wife Gayle and I got to meet President Ford at a small reception in Alexandria, Virginia. His former neighbors hosted it. Gerald Ford was a compassionate, honest and kind man. Sadly, he will only be remembered for pardoning our 37th President and thus saving this country from a painful legal proceeding.

Each year, the money from the sale of White House Christmas ornaments at

Rankin's was given to the Warrenton Lion's Club for their charity efforts. Jim Rankin also participated in the Jaycees Christmas Toy Workshop and the Shop With A Cop program. It was not unusual for him to donate brand new bicycles and other toys for poor children living in Fauquier County.

In an age where small businesses are being forced to close because of mega stores like Costco, Home Depot and Loews's, I always found what I needed at Rankin's. What I experienced was friendly and knowledgeable employees, reasonable prices and a thank you for my purchases. I left the store with a smile on my face.

Customers wrote reviews like, "Great place also really helpful staff," "Rankin's is truly a wonderful, friendly, efficient neighborhood store. Generally have everything we need for everyday projects at a reasonable price. Their sales are an added bonus." And, "Always have what we need."

Rankin's Hardware had been successful because everyone working at the stores in Colonial Beach, King George, Warrenton and Winchester had embraced Jim Rankin's philosophy that, "Service at True Value Hardware is old-fashioned but the inventory is completely modern. Good customer business relationships."

Regrettably, in this life, even the best stores eventually close their doors or are sold to other larger companies. On March 30, 2021, the Rankin family that included Alvin Rankin, Beverly and Loyd Alspaugh and Alice and Mike Kniceley issued a one-page letter stating, "We are pleased to announced Rankin's True Value Hardware will now become ACE Hardware." The next day, the three stores in Colonial Beach, King George and Warrenton became Costello's Ace Hardware. It was the end of an important business empire.

Vinnie Costello of Deer Park, New York had founded ACE Hardware in 1973. At the end of 2022, it had hardware stores in 46 locations in Maryland, New Jersey, New York, Pennsylvania and Virginia. The company's goal is to have 75 stores and $250 million dollars in sales by 2025.

At the time of the sale, Jim Rankin noted, "I don't own any part of it any longer. I gave it all to the children, and I don't know what all they got going on. I've heard bits and parts." In a wise move, the new company retained Kent Rankin as the hardware store manager.

In a Facebook posting on February 21, 2022 referring to the upcoming sale, a family representative wrote, "It was a great run started in 1966. 55 years. Thank you to everyone that worked for us and did business with us. All of our friends and neighbors and fellow business owners are and will always be very special to our family. Thank you to mom and dad for all the opportunity you gave us to succeed." This was a very classy statement.

While Jim Rankin may not have been involved in the hardware stores, he wasn't about to retire. In fact, in 1992, he decided to not only open a furniture store but to buy the Waterloo Station Shopping Center from a Maryland based Chevy Chase Corporation. These 2.5 acres of land on Waterloo Street in Warrenton had been the previous site of an Acme Grocery

Store, Gill's Tractor Dealership and the Pennsylvania House furniture store.

When he took possession of what became the Rankin's Waterloo Shopping Center, Joe and Vinnie's Pizza owned by Sharron and Vincenzo Giambanco had already been established. They are still selling tasty pizzas and subs.

On June 9, 1992, Rankin's Furniture was open for business. When asked why he decided to operate a furniture store, Jim Rankin responded, "It kind of just happened. Every shopping center needs an anchor store." His 31,500 square foot furniture shop soon became that anchor. Two days later, Jim Rankin told Susette Ritenour with the *Fauquier Times Democrat,* "You have to give credit to your employees. They've really stayed with me. They, too, are part of the reason I decided to do this."

According to the reporter, "He praised his family, his wife Shirley, sons Alvin and Glenn, daughters Beverly Alspaugh and Alice Kniceley, Beverly's husband Loyd, Alice's husband Mike and his brother Charles for supporting him in his latest bold move."

While the original plan was to move the True Value Hardware to the Rankin's Waterloo Shopping Center, this merger didn't occur. At the time, Jim Rankin noted, "I still have two years on my lease, so I'm not ready to make a decision."

Throughout his career, Jim Rankin has advertised extensively throughout the Washington metropolitan area. His basic message, "The Store carries a wide variety of living room and dining room furniture, beds and bedroom furniture, and accessories." He added, "I think a lot of people think there is a lot of profit in it. But there's not. Furniture is a tough business. We carry only quality furniture."

Over the years, Rankin's Furniture has sold world-class handcrafted products manufactured by Barcalounger, Best, Brookside, England, Flexsteel, Franklin, Howard Miller and Temple. Most of the furniture in my living room was made by the England Furniture Company of New Tazewell, Tennessee.

Each of these beautiful, comfortable and well-built chairs was purchased from the Rankin's Furniture Store.

Even our cats have enjoyed sleeping in them and you can count me as one of the legends of Rankin's satisfied customers. If there is ever a problem with delivery or product quality, Jim Rankin will personally fix the problem.

In the spring of 2007, Jim Rankin decided to sell the Waterloo Shopping Center. According to Andrea Ferrero, who along with his wife Amber, are the owners of Café Torino, Mr. Rankin knocked on his business door and announced, "I have a proposed contract to buy the shopping center. You have 60 days to match the offer." Without hesitation, Amber Ferrero said, "We will take it. "

On May 27, 2007, the Ferrero's, along with some close friends and investors, acquired the shopping center and formed the ABC&J Limited Liability Company. Café Torino had served excellent Northern Italian cuisine and pastries since it opened on May 14, 2001. During our conversation, Andrea opined,

"They affectionately refer to Mr. Jim Rankin as Napoleon. He is short, demanding, a very straight shooter and a phenomenal businessman."

In this age of excruciating, mind numbing and boring television advertising, Jim Rankin has become a local media celebrity. In order to sell products in today's hyper competitive market, a salesman must capture the attention of a prospective customer and motivate then to turn off their iPhone, get off the coach, drive their car and visit your store.

Jim Rankin has produced a number of catchy, effective and entertaining 30-second commercials. My favorite begins with Mr. Rankin dressed up as the Virginia Revolutionary patriot Patrick Henry. He is holding a lamp and telling his audience, "The savings are coming. The savings are coming at Rankin's Furniture. We have Flexsteel, England, Howard Miller clocks and curios, and Hekman Office Furniture. This place is huge. We have dining room and living room sets. We have a huge collection of recliners too. One if by land, two as by sea, you can get

20 percent off when you come see me. Rankin's Furniture looks small on the outside but it is huge inside."

A second television commercial recaptures Jim Rankin's heroic service to this county. It starts with the tag line: "Stop into Rankin's Furniture for quality furniture and outstanding customer service." As you continue to watch the ad, an Army C-119 flying boxcar plane appears. At the rear of the plane, Sergeant James Rankin is dressed in his highly decorated Army uniform. He then jumps out of the plane.

During his airborne service in Korea, Sergeant Rankin had the responsibility of ensuring that each of his men was ready to leave the plane when the light changed from red to green. For those who hesitated, it was his job as the "pusher" to encourage their timely departure. Even a few seconds can mean the difference between making and missing your assigned landing site.

After successfully making it to the ground in the commercial, he says, "Wow. Rankin's Furniture has a beautiful collection. Celebrate Rankin's 24th Anniversary Sale. Spin to win gifts and discounts on your purchase. No pressure sales." The television ad ends with Mr. Rankin stating, "Boy made it again."

A third commercial finds Jim Rankin pretending to be asleep on a brown Flexsteel couch. His first words are, "Oh Gee. I must have went to sleep. Come try this new Flexsteel sofa and you will go to sleep too." You then hear the announcer say, "Choose from Flexsteel, England, Catnapper, Jackson, Von Bassett, Stein World and more." Mr. Rankin ends the commercial with, "Quality furniture, outstanding customer service, great prices, Rankin's Furniture."

These advertisements have appeared on various television stations and can still be enjoyed on YouTube. Unlike the non-stop pleas to buy certain health products, car insurance or pillows, the Rankin commercials are a pleasure to watch because they are amusing, informative, timeless and unique. He doesn't use paid actors or testimonials from people who will try to convince you that only their product will allow you to discover the elusive fountain of youth.

In addition to television advertising, Jim Rankin has always embraced the local print and online media. He pays for a weekly print ad in *The Fauquier Times.* In these pieces, he writes, "Being in business for over 60 years, I have always found *The Fauquier Times* to be a useful tool for total audience reach." He added, "The majority of our furniture customers don't live in Fauquier County." There are a number of satisfied folks who would agree with his assessment.

Deb P of East Falmouth, Massachusetts wrote, "Surprising selection for a small-town furniture store. Excellent in-store service and helpful delivery personnel. Bought a nice piece for our family room. Will shop there again."

Beth B of Ardmore, Pennsylvania opined, "We wanted a specific chair in a specific fabric and Rankin's was the only place in the DC area that carried it. We drove out to Warrenton from Fairfax and they remembered my husband calling about the chair and getting a quote on the price. We met Mr. Rankin and felt great about supporting a family business with great customer service."

Erin B of Warrenton, Virginia noted, "As someone who has lived my entire life in Fauquier County, I have long admired Mr. Rankin. During the past decade, I have purchased chairs and sofas from his Warrenton store. The quality, price and service have been outstanding. I always recommend this store to family and friends. It is worth the trip to Warrenton." In response to these and many other positive reviews, Jim Rankin responded, "I want to thank the public for patronizing us. The people have been good to us. We have good customer relations."

Jim Rankin is a business survivor. According to the U.S Small Business Administration about 550,00 small businesses close each year. Many did not survive the COVID lock-downs. Those who did, like Rankin's Furniture, now face multiple threats.

Small businesses are dealing with the two-headed monster of inflation and rising interest rates. It is becoming increasingly difficult and expensive for them to obtain the necessary capital to keep their doors open.

Dozens of brick-and-mortar stores are going broke because they simply can't compete with Amazon, COSCO, EBay, Wal-Mart and online companies. Some years ago, Jim Rankin told *The Fauquier Times,* "The big companies are coming in and running the little companies out of business." Fauquier County's small businesses have not been spared in this process.

Since I moved here nearly 40 years ago, I have witnessed the demise of local popular stores such as the Ames Department Store, Ben Franklin's, Blue Ridge Hardware, Carter's General Store, Jamesway, Leggett's, Pebbles, the Rhodes Drug Store and the Southern Department Store. The reasons for their closing vary.

While progress is inevitable, for millions of small businesses throughout the United States, it has been a painful experience. Instead of buying products from our neighbors; today's consumers are using computers, tablets and IPhones to order items from faceless and nameless merchants.

In the commercial sales world there are a number of keys to long-term success. Among them are the tried and true axioms such as, "The customer is always right" and "Treating customers the way they want to be treated." Jim Rankin has followed this sage advice for the past 57 years. This philosophy works. How many times have you called a company with a complaint or question and had to spend what seemed like an eternity dealing with a non-responsive computer or someone who just learned the English language. You can avoid all that chaos by shopping at your hometown stores.

Since 2006, *The Warrenton Lifestyle Magazine* and the online *Fauquier Now* have encouraged the citizens of Fauquier County to vote on a broad range of categories. These have included artists, entertainment, farm equipment, food and beverages, home services and pet services.

Since its inception, county residents have voted for Rankin's Furniture and Rankin's Hardware as the "Best of Fauquier County" for 12 of the 18 years. In its most recent success, *The Fauquier Now* announced, "Your votes have indicated that Rankin's Furniture is the best place to get your furniture shopping in-town. This locally owned family business has been serving the community for over 25 years and offers casual, elegant, modern and eclectic options to suit any design."

For the past seven years, *The Fauquier Times* has conducted its own Reader's Choice Contest. Those living in the community could vote for the Best Arts and Entertainment, Best Automotive, Best Home and Garden, Best Food and Drinks, Best Public Servants, Best Professional Services and Best Shopping. For this entire period, including 2023, Rankin's Furniture has won the Readers Choice Award. This is an impressive accomplishment.

Jim Rankin has always been a superb businessman and generous contributor to worthy causes throughout

Fauquier County. He is a lifelong member of the Fauquier Chamber of Commerce and the Rotary Club. Over the years, he has financially supported the Booster Clubs of Fauquier, Kettle Run and Liberty High Schools, Boy Scouts of America, Fauquier County Boys and Girls Club, Fauquier County Parks and Recreation, the Jaycees, New Baltimore and Warrenton Lions Club, the Shop with a Cop Christmas Program and sponsored various local sports teams.

According to the former Chief of the Warrenton Volunteer Fire Company, Dale Koglin, Jim Rankin was once an Associate Member of the company who enjoyed calling the bingo numbers at their weekly game. He also never hesitated to donate various items for the Fire Company's annual Carnival that provided wholesome entertainment for over 60 years. It was the first fireman's carnival in Fauquier County and it was always a glorious time for country residents.

Jim Rankin was also doing his part to save our planet long before recycling became fashionable. In the October 1991 edition of *The Fauquier Magazine,* writer

David Chuse told his readers, "Rankin's hardware cut its trash output by 75 percent through recycling cardboard." Sadly, this fine magazine, co-published by Ellen and Lawrence Emerson, stopped producing *The Fauquier Magazine* in 1997.

In 2002, Jim Rankin was selected by the Small Business Development Center of Fauquier County as the local Small Business Veteran of the Year.

Two decades later on November 5, 2022, he was presented with the Business Person of the Year Award. The Fauquier Chamber of Commerce annually gives this recognition. Local Fauquier County delegate Michael Webert, who was a co-founder of the Business Development Caucus in the Virginia House of Delegates, bestowed this honor to Mr. Rankin.

On June 21, 2023, Jim Rankin took out a full-page advertisement in *The Fauquier Times* announcing his "Independence Day Sale." The message was, "Hurry! Score Star Spangled Savings on the entire Flexsteel line." It was an effective pitch with color pictures of

Flexsteel products, a patriotic marching band and a tribute to the American flag representing our great and noble country.

Finally, unlike other Virginia counties, like Arlington, Fairfax and Loudoun, there is currently no "Hall of Fame" for local businessmen and businesswomen. This is something that hopefully will soon be established.

Without question, a charter member of that organization should be Jim Rankin. His business motto of, "Quality Products, Outstanding Customer Services, Great Prices and Caring about the people who live in the community," should be an inspiration to anyone who contemplates selling products to the general public.

As of this writing, there are four dedicated individuals, Mike Fraley, Jim Hadler, Tom Hadler and Ann Jenkins who assist Jim Rankin in the sale of his outstanding furniture products.

If you add the time spent at the hardware and furniture stores just counting Mr. Rankin, his four children and their spouses, collectively they have more than 250 years of experience selling products to the general public. There were also at least 15 blood relatives who gained life experiences working at one or both of these flagship stores. This is a truly memorable story and one of the best examples I have ever heard of a family owned business.

I look forward to the day when the Fauquier Chamber of Commerce bestows Hall of Fame status on James Alvin Rankin. He is a remarkable small businessman.

Chapter 7: A Life Well Lived

As a child growing up in Fauquier County, spring was a magical time for Jimmy Rankin. It was about getting the fields ready for planting, taking care of the farm animals and looking forward to the first sandlot baseball game of the new year.

Some of Jimmy Rankin's most prized possessions were his well-used baseball glove and his trusty wooden bat. Baseball was America's pastime and an opportunity for him to put aside the daily struggles of farm life during the Great Depression and World War II. For just a few brief moments, he could dream about being Ty Cobb, Babe Ruth or local Washington Senators favorite, Walter "The Big Train" Johnson.

Baseball is a simple but magnificent game. You don't need to be 6'5, 300 pounds or able to skate 15-miles-per-hour on ice to be successful. You simply needed a ball, bat and a place to play. Jimmy Rankin loved to test himself against his brothers and neighbor kids on a baseball diamond. It was here where he could hit a 5-ounch-horsehide ball a country mile.

Jim Rankin never lost his love of the game. Upon returning from Korea, he managed a local adult baseball team in Catlett, Virginia. On May 3, 1963, the first night game under the lights took place at Benner Field located at the then Warrenton High School. There were seven teams in the Northern Virginia League representing Bristersburg, Catlett, Hume, Manassas, Nokesville, The Plains and Warrenton. Members of the Metropolitan Umpire Association officiated the games.

It was a long season of about 17 games per team were played throughout the summer. The top four teams advanced to the playoffs in September. According to legendary local *Fauquier Democrat* sports writer, Alan A. Poe, "The schedule in the future is very promising and should mean some very good baseball for the fans and good gates for the league. From the players standpoint the night games are going over big."

During the 1963 baseball campaign, Jim Rankin's Catlett squad was having a great deal of success on the field. He had a number of talented local players such as Jake Allen, Doug and Norman Chewning, Lester Day, Otis Deal, Billy Frazier, Jesse Jenkins, Wayne Martin, Doug Meadows, Frank Riley, Robert Sisson, David Lee Stanley, Doug Stanley and Boo Walls.

The team's outstanding center fielder Jesse Lee Jenkins had just completed his military service as a radio operator in the United States Army. He played a baseball game for Catlett a week before he married his beautiful bride, Ann Elizabeth Kline of Bealeton, at the Midland Church of the Brethren. This is the same Ann Jenkins who has worked with Jim Rankin for over a half century.

In his last game as a bachelor, Jesse Jenkins was an integral part of a 17-hit attack against the previously unbeaten Nokesville Rebels. This was Nokesville's first loss after winning 12 consecutive games over two seasons. Catlett's winning pitcher in the 7 to 3 decision was David Lee Stanley.

In that same month, Catlett had a game against The Plains Hillbillies. According to Alan Poe, who spent 53 years working for his hometown newspaper, "Catlett went on a hitting binge at The Plains Sunday and knocked the corn squeezum out of the Hillbillies to the tune of 18 to 8."

During the period of these adult baseball games, most players did not arrive at the games with a cooler full of drinks or Yeti tumblers. Instead, their thirst was quenched by the generosity of local soft drink distributors Nehi and Pepsi-Cola. Jesse James of the Nehi Bottling Company always had enough delicious cold orange and grape sodas for the players. These gifts were always appreciated.

In September of 1963, the Bristersburg Express in a semi-final game defeated Catlett. It was a sad ending to a successful season. This grief was magnified two months later, when John Fitzgerald Kennedy was assassinated in Dallas, Texas. President Kennedy had long championed the idea of individuals volunteering for worthy causes. He once said, "One person can make a difference and everyone should try." Jim Rankin has been making a difference his entire life. While he was unable to join the Boy Scouts of America during the Great Depression and World War II, he has always been a strong supporter of the Piedmont District Scouting Program.

Jim Rankin has often served as a member of the Eagle Review Board. Many of those who achieved this most prestigious award in scouting became prominent members of American society. Among the most famous are: our 38th President Gerald R. Ford, NASA astronaut and first man on the Moon, Neil Armstrong, J. Willard Marriott, Jr., Steven Spielberg and Jimmy Stewart.

For nearly 20 years, the Rankin's True Value Hardware Store provided space in their parking lot for the sale of Boy Scout Christmas trees. As someone who has volunteered to sell these trees in the past, I can attest that this is the largest annual fundraiser for Boy Scout Troops in Fauquier County.

In recognition of all of his efforts, Jim Rankin was presented on October 15, 2015 with the Roland Tapscott Fauquier Good Scout Award. He became the second recipient of this prestigious award named for his brother-in-arms Roland Tapscott.

When the original award was given posthumously to the family of Roland Tapscott, Kathryn Kulick, Chairwoman of the Piedmont District Boy Scouts noted, "The Boy Scouts of America is, above all, a young man's character and leadership program. We cannot imagine a better and more humble role model for our young men than Roland Tapscott."
Other recipients of this award are Fauquier County Superintendent of Schools, Dr. Major Warner, local philanthropist Ralph Crafts and Fire Chief of the Fauquier County Fire and Rescue, Darren Stevens.

In addition to supporting the Boy Scouts, Jim Rankin has always championed veteran's causes. As a Korean War veteran, he understands how war can radically change its survivors both mentally and physically. Many are scarred for life. Jim Rankin helped many of these folks. In the words of his dear friend, Roland Tapscott, "Jim Rankin will take the shirt off his back for someone who needs help. I think he just wants to give back to the community. I've seen him do unbelievable things for people who walk into his store asking for help." Some of these folks were veterans.

In recognition of his heroic military service, then Secretary of Defense Robert M. Gates sent Jim Rankin a Certificate of Appreciation. This document says, "In recognition of honorable service during the Korean War in defense of democracy and freedom. Through your selfless sacrifice, the tide of communism on the Korean Peninsula was halted and liberty triumphed over tyranny. The Department of Defense and the people of America and Korea are forever grateful."

Robert Gates was a Second Lieutenant in the United States Air Force who became a career intelligence officer. President Ronald Reagan appointed him Director of the Central Intelligence Agency in 1987. He became our nation's 22nd Secretary of Defense and served in that vital capacity in both the George W.

Bush and Barrack Obama
Administrations. Robert Gates received
the Presidential Medal of Freedom Award
in 2011.

Jim Rankin also received a
Certificate of Honor from the IKE
Eisenhower Foundation. This
organization was established in 1945 in
Abilene, Kansas to honor the leadership,
life and incredible legacy of our 34th
President, Dwight David Eisenhower. In
our nation's history only Henry Arnold,
Omar Bradley, Dwight D. Eisenhower,
Douglas MacArthur and George C.
Marshall were five star Generals of the
United States Army. Of these American
heroes, only Eisenhower became
President.

In the IKE Foundation award, it
says, "Mr. James A. Rankin, Sr. Has been a
champion of the life and legacy of Dwight
D. Eisenhower and is hereby presented
with this Certificate of Honor. " The Chair
of the Board of Directors Mary Jean
Eisenhower and the Executive Director
Meredith Sleichter signed the document.

Jim Rankin has long lamented that most Americans have little, if any, knowledge of what happened in the early 1950's on the Korean Peninsula. This bloody conflict lasted 1,097 days and cost the lives of 36,574 American soldiers who made the ultimate sacrifice on faraway battlefields for this country. He will always honor the lives of these brave heroes and the 103,284 Americans wounded and the 4,714 prisoners of war. Many of these men never returned to their loved ones.

The American people may have no memory of our "Forgotten War" but Jim Rankin will never forget the extraordinary sacrifices under some of the most brutal conditions.

Since leaving the Fauquier County Board of Supervisors in 1998, Jim Rankin has largely stayed out of local politics. While never missing an opportunity to vote in a primary or general election, his independent political spirit still burns brightly. On April 18, 2019, he decided to publicly express his support for Fauquier County's 60th Sheriff.

In his letter printed in *The Fauquier Times,* Jim Rankin opined, "I have known many of our Sheriffs. And as a former county Supervisor, I have worked closely with some. Unequivocally, Bob Mosier has been the best Sheriff of Fauquier County I have seen in my lifetime, and has accomplished more in three years than some Sheriffs have in over 20."

He concluded the letter entitled: "In Sheriff Mosier, we have the best" by stating, "We've got a Sheriff with a very impressive list of accomplishments. Let's not change Sheriffs now. The winner of this primary will face no opposition in the November election. So please, it's important that you join me at the primary on June 11 and re-elect Bob Mosier as our Sheriff."

Since being re-elected in 2019, Robert "Bob" Mosier has served the citizens of Virginia with distinction as Sheriff of Fauquier County, Virginia Secretary of Public Safety and Homeland Security and now Chief Deputy, Administrative and Corrections Bureau, Loudoun County Sheriff's Office. He has dedicated more than 30 years protecting the lives and property of all of us living in the Commonwealth.

During a recent conversation about James Alvin Rankin, Sr., Bob said, "I am truly honored to be writing this message to recognize the tremendous impact that Jim Rankin has had on Fauquier County. When I met him in the 1990s, as a deputy sheriff working with then Sheriff Ashby Olinger, I was immediately struck by his commitment to family, community, and business. His nine years on the Board of Supervisors was one of hard work, commitment and dedication to his constituents. He was always an independent voice for Fauquier County.

"Over the years, I have been privileged to witness first-hand the embodiment of his values: fairness, truth, justice, and the American way. He has been an influential presence in many of our meetings, always expressing his views in a meaningful manner. His achievements are celebrated by the entire community, who support his businesses in recognition of his leadership and good citizenship.

"As I look to the future, I hope to emulate Jim Rankin's example and continue the legacy of service and dedication that he continues to leave in Fauquier County."

In 2013, the newly created Fauquier Veterans Bridge Council was persuaded by Jim Rankin to consider naming a bridge in Warrenton after his beloved and highly decorated father, Clay Preston Rankin. Retired U.S. Navy combat veteran Jay Pinsky established this organization. It was his idea to honor those county residents who heroically fought for this country. The membership of the Bridge Council included military veterans and volunteers.

While there are many bridges and heroes in Fauquier County, Silver Star recipient Private First Class Clay Rankin was a worthy candidate. As a member of the American Legion, Jim Rankin was able to convince the Bridge Board to approve his selection and submit it to the Fauquier County Board of Supervisors.

As a former distinguished member of the Board of Supervisors, Jim Rankin spearheaded this important naming recognition. On November 13, 2014, Mr. Rankin was rewarded for his effective lobbying efforts. The five supervisors, Christopher Granger, Peter B. Schwartz, Lee Sherbeyn, Chester Stribling and Holder Trumbo voted unanimously to submit the petition to the Commonwealth of Virginia's Transportation Board asking that the Meetze Road Bridge be named the "Private First Class Clay Preston Rankin USA Bridge." The petition noted, "Private First Class Rankin was awarded the Silver Star for displaying remarkable courage and devotion in the front line through heavy machine gun fire."

On February 18, 2015, the Commonwealth Transportation Board in Richmond, Virginia agreed to the Board of Supervisors request. On June 8, 2015, the Fauquier Veterans Bridge Council unveiled the new name for the Meetze Road Bridge over Routes 29 and 17 in Warrenton. It is now called the "PFC Clay Rankin Memorial Bridge." In attendance at this ceremony were Jim Rankin, Charlie Rankin, Clayborne Rankin III, Supervisor Lee Sherbeyn, Council creator, Jay Pinsky and his family.

In addition to the Rankin Bridge, the Fauquier Veterans Bridge Council was able to rename the Opal Bypass Bridge after William Sidney Shacklette. As a member of the United States Navy, Bob Shacklette of Delaplane, Virginia was a hospital steward on the U.S.S. Bennington. The boilers on this ship exploded in San Diego harbor on July 21, 1905. Despite third-degree burns over much of his body, Seaman Shacklette saved the lives of many of his fellow sailors. He was awarded the Medal of Honor. Since 2014, motorists now use the "William Sidney Shacklette Bypass."

The third bridge naming occurred in Remington, Virginia on March 7, 2018. The recipient was U.S. Army Technical Sgt. Harold Davis. This World War II hero fought his way across Europe and earned a Bronze Star, four Purple Hearts and other commendations. The bridge that was named TSGT Harold J. Davis, U.S. Army, Memorial Bridge had been constructed in 2013 and been previously known as the Tinpot Run Bridge.

In addition to honoring his father's heroic achievements in the First World

War, Jim Rankin is immensely proud of his wife of almost 70 years, Shirley and their four children, eight grandchildren, 17 great grandchildren and two great great grandchildren. One of their grandsons even became an airborne paratrooper.

In 2000, grandson Todd Alspaugh enlisted in the United States Army. He is the son of Loyd and Beverly Rankin Alspaugh of Colonial Beach, Virginia. They managed the Rankin's True Value Hardware Store in that town for 30 years. Beverly and her brother Alvin still own the Peddlers Market in Colonial Beach that has about 90 boutique shops selling antiques, art, crafts, collectibles, pottery and upscale furniture.

After serving a tour of duty, Todd Alspaugh decided to become an Assistant Manager at the Rankin's True Value Hardware Store in King George, Virginia. Alvin Rankin managed this business. While he enjoyed working at the family owned store, with the memory of the 9-11 attack and the War in Iraqi, Todd decided to re-enlist in the United States Army. After completing training at Fort Bragg,

North Carolina, Todd became a proud member of the "All American Division." The 82nd Airborne has a proud tradition of fighting in nearly every American engagement including World War I, World War II, Dominican Republic, Vietnam, Grenada, Panama, Persian Gulf War, Haiti, Bosnia, Iraq and Afghanistan. Their colorful mottos are: "All the Way" and "Death From Above."

During his 20-years of outstanding service to this great country, now Chief Warrant Officer Level 3 Todd Alspaugh had been deployed to Kuwait, Korea and three tours of Afghanistan. While in the United States, he spent three years working at the Aberdeen Proving Grounds in Maryland. He took numerous courses in cyber security and rose to become a Professor. Like his grandfather, he will always be a proud paratrooper.

During one of my first visits with Jim Rankin, he told me the reason he survived the hellish battles in Korea was because of the prayers of his beloved mother, Naomi Rankin. His long time pastor at the Midland Church of the Brethren, Rev. Tim Monn opined, "He's a fellow who's been very successful in business, but is very modest. He believes he has received so much so he can help others. He helps people in trouble find strength. He sets a very high standard for himself, but does not pull away from people who fall short of those standards. He draws them closer. He has been triumphant over every adversity he has experienced. He credits his mother and the church. He's very fervent about his faith."

During the last few months, the Midland Church of the Brethren had a fund raising event for disaster relief victims throughout the world. Despite high interest rates and soaring consumer prices, the congregation donated about $1000 for this effort. According to one of its members, Jim Rankin, without fanfare, said he would match this amount.

In terms of family, Jim Rankin has been a great son, father and grandfather. The Rankin's stores became successful because of not only Jim Rankin's tireless efforts but also those of his children and grandchildren. This group alone has more than 250 years of experience selling furniture and hardware to the general public. There were even cousins and nephews who were part of the heartbeat of this business empire.

For the Rankin family it was always more than just working together. Most members of the family are parishioners of the Midland Church of the Brethren. Prior to their passing, the entire Rankin clan would meet each month at the home of Clay and Naomi Rankin. These dinners were moved to the houses of their offspring.

Each summer, a Sunday would be set-aside for the Rankin family reunion party. A favorite spot for these festivities was the Bull Run Regional Park in Manassas, Virginia. At least one member of the family would arrive early to rent a pavilion for the family. Rankin family members arrived from Maryland, Pennsylvania, Virginia and West Virginia.

While there was always plenty of barbeque, chicken, fellowship, hamburgers and hot dogs, most attendees look forward to the annual softball game. Everyone young and old participated in these games and the competition to win could be fierce.

Sadly, there are many in America who are unable to attend or have family reunions for a variety of reasons. The Rankin family is unusual because for the past one hundred years they have been able to keep their family together despite wars, Great Depressions and political upheavals.

Ann Jenkins, who is Jim Rankin's second cousin wrote, "Mr. Rankin hired me on the spot in March of 1970 to work at Rankin's Hardware. I've been there for his many business ventures including opening additional hardware stores, purchasing of Rankin's Waterloo Shopping Center and opening Rankin's Furniture in 1992. He's such a fair, kind-hearted and giving person to his employees, to his community and to anyone he meets.

He's given me so many opportunities to travel and buy merchandise for the stores. I've been around him the majority of my life and I've seen that he's the same person towards everyone. I've worked with him so long that we think alike. I've had 53 enjoyable years being his right hand person. I look forward to continuing to work for him until he retires."

Nephew Kent Rankin noted, "Jim Rankin is a hardnosed, no nonsense man who is loyal and fair to everyone especially those who worked for him. Extremely loyal and an incredible businessman."

Local small businessman and owner of Tom Frost Firestone, Dave A. Jenkins opined, "Jim has been a real community man for many years the likes of which we may never see again. Good friend and great customer."

In terms of his public service to the Fauquier County community, Jim Rankin's campaign manager, Rich Galecki opined, "To have someone like that in public service is pretty rare. A lot of people have an agenda. I don't think Jim has a personal agenda, he has a Fauquier County agenda."

Another outstanding public servant, Gail Barb recently wrote, "James Rankin (Jim to all his friends) is a lifelong resident of Fauquier County with family roots that run deep through Fauquier. A true patriot who served his country. Jim is a very successful businessman with several family owned stores that he and his family have managed and worked in themselves for many years.

"When I first ran for political office in 1999 for Clerk of Fauquier County Circuit Court, Jim was one of the first people to show support and encouragement for my campaign. He is a kind and very generous man." Gail Barb has served the people of Fauquier County with the highest distinction.

The current Center District Supervisor, Kevin Carter describes Jim Rankin, "As a Virginia gentleman. He is a loyal patriot, family man and businessman. He embodies what it is to be a good citizen by his intense participation in our community. From service in the Korean War, serving as an elected official and volunteering countless hours to community organizations including the Rotary Club where we met for the first time.

Mr. Rankin is a hero in my mind and a man of his character doesn't come along often enough. Thank you Mr. Rankin for being a bright shining star for the rest of us to emulate."

Long time Fauquier County Lee District Supervisor, Chris Butler of Remington stated, "I was 16 years old and my dad said I needed a job. I asked mom if she'd take me to Rankin's Hardware so I could see if they were hiring. I knew Mr. Rankin through our mutual friend, Ashby Olinger, who was our Sheriff. I went in and Mr. Rankin invited me into his office and said, 'What can I do for you Governor?

"I asked him for a job, we agreed on the rate of pay. As I was leaving his office he said to me 'Now I 'm not going to pay you to talk to people, I expect you to work.' I agreed and during my time under his employ, he asked me several times if I was running for office, as I talked to everyone that came in. He knew long before I did that I would serve my community. To this day Mr. Rankin calls me Governor and I call him the same. He was a mentor to me and is my good friend today!"

Lifelong Fauquier County resident and former candidate for County Sheriff, Roger Beavers of The Plains succinctly opined, "Jim Rankin is a good man."

There were also members of the American Legion who described Jim Rankin in glowing terms. Robert "Bob" Brady who has held a number of leadership positions in Post 72 in Warrenton and Post 247 in Remington stated, "Jim Rankin is a long time member of the American Legion. He has served as a mentor to many young members and he was instrumental in obtaining a loan for the building of Post 72. Over the years, Jim served on numerous Veterans Committees and is a highly knowledgeable member of the American Legion."

During one of our many conversations, I asked Mr. Rankin to highlight some of his most favorite things. Not surprisingly, he said his favorite book is *Rakkasan, The 187th Airborne Regimental Combat Team in Korea.* His hero is his father, Silver Star recipient Clayborne P. Rankin. Favorite song is Amazing Grace and his sage advice is, "Do what you do, right the first time and you won't have to do it again." This was a saying frequently used by his parents, Clay and Naomi Rankin. I once asked him, who was his best friend. He replied, "Everyone is my friend."

Among his golden rules are: "Every parent should have the right to leave a piece of land for their children to live on." "Reach out. Help Somebody. Work together." "Always treat people the way you want to be treated. The key to success in a community is good Customer-Business relationships."

Tradition, commitment, family and faith have been at the core of James Alvin Rankin's world for over 90 years. He dearly loves his wife, Shirley, his children and many grandchildren. Oldest son, Alvin Rankin said, "He taught me everything I know." Daughter Beverly Rankin Alspaugh opined, "He is always there when anyone whether it be a relative or not needs him." His youngest daughter, Alice perhaps summed it up best, when asked to describe her father, she simply said, "He is a great man."

Alice recalled an incident that occurred on Christmas Eve in 1977. It was closing time and everyone was anxious to get home. Before locking the front door, a lady approached the store. In Alice's words, "He let this woman go through the toy section and pick out toys for her two grandkids. He gave them to her. That is when I really, as a young teen, saw his compassion for people."

In Jim Rankin's life, "God, Family and County" are the three most important things. Jim Rankin is an American patriot. Jim Rankin's life has been dedicated to military service, public service and customer service. Irish playwright, George Bernard Shaw famously wrote, "A gentleman is one who puts more into the world than he takes out."

This accurately describes James Alvin Rankin who has lived a meaningful and well-lived life!

ACKNOWLEDGEMENTS

During the past decade, I have written three books about important local public figures that have made significant contributions to Fauquier County, Virginia. These include: *The People's Sheriff, A Century of Keeping the Peace* and now *Rankin's Place: A Story of a Hero and Community Leader.* James Alvin Rankin is a living legend in Fauquier County and his life story is not only interesting but a remarkable one about patriotic service, public service and customer service.

During our first meeting, I told Jim Rankin I was interested in writing a book about him. He responded, "Why do you want to do a book on me?" After a few moments of reflection, I said, you have led an extraordinary life and your friends, neighbors and the American people need to know about your achievements in the United States military, your public service to the community and your small business empire. I would like to be the storyteller but you, Jim Rankin, are the story!

Throughout 2023, I would drive to Rankin's Furniture Store, without an appointment, to meet with Mr. Rankin. Despite being on the clock, he was always more than willing to grant me access to all of his files and graciously answers each and every one of my questions. We tried to meet at least every other week. What I learned in this process was that Jim Rankin is a humble, kind, soft spoken, witty and a man with a remarkable memory. We developed a rapport and I hope friendship.

It has been a great honor to write this book. I would also like to extend my gratitude and appreciation to Alvin Rankin, Beverly Rankin Aspaugh, Alice Rankin Kniceley, Mike Kniceley and Bryan Kniceley. Bryan has been the family conduit for this project and the author of the excellently written Foreword tribute to James Alvin Rankin, Sr.

I would like to acknowledge the assistance of Gail Barg, Roger Beavers, Bob Brady, Chris Bulter, Kevin Carter, Rich Galecki, Dave A. Jenkins, Captain Mark Jones of the Fauquier County Sheriff's Office, Rev. Tim Monn, Lt. Col.

Robert Mosier of the Loudoun County Sheriff's Office, Kent Rankin and Roland Tapscott for providing inspiriting tributes and quotes found in this book.

Special thanks to Ann Jenkins who has tirelessly worked for Mr. Rankin since 1970 as his right-hand person and who was an invaluable resource for this book. Many thanks for your kindness.

In addition, I want to thank Renee C. Culbertson, Deputy Municipal Clerk to the Board of Supervisors, Buddy Holmes, Jay Pinsky, Frank Ramey, Matthew Smith and one of Fauquier County's finest historians, John Toler for their valuable contributions to this book. In Fauquier County, we are blessed to not only have three of the best public libraries in the Commonwealth of Virginia but one of the finest group of library professionals who are always dedicated, helpful, kind and knowledgeable. I want, in particular, to thank Jeanne Day, Daryl Jackson, Pam Lovera, Allison Pruntel and Dawn Sowers. I spent nearly 100 hours in the Virginiana Room at the Warrenton Public Library and this book would not have been successful without their assistance, kindness and patience.

A second group that was invaluable to me on this book and many others is my Writing Group. Twice a month, they provide me with important insights and suggestions. They give me the motivation to keep writing and to stick to a schedule. Many warm thanks to Anita Metzger and Joy Schaya. For this book, my dear friend Joy Schaya has once again agreed to spend hours reading, editing and improving this biography. She is an outstanding writer of Children's and Young Adult books and I am so grateful to her.

To my son, Chris, who has been my partner for the past eight self-published books, you are an essential part of any success that I have achieved or will in the future. I may write the words but Chris is responsible for ensuring people can read them. Without his many contributions, my books would simply be words written in pencil on a yellow legal pad. Thank you for making all of my books a reality.

Finally, none of my books would have been written without the counsel, patience and understanding of my beautiful wife, Gayle. We are blessed to have a wonderful life together with our sons Rick and Chris, their wives Erin and Stacey and our precious grandchildren Mitchell, Elise, Kelly, Christopher and Connor.

Silas Clatterbuck.

Sergueant, France,
Dec. 9, 1918.

Dear father:—

I will try and write you a few lines this beautiful sabbath day. These few lines leaves me feeling fine and dandy. Hope you are the same. I have not heard anything from any of the folks at home for a long time, but guess you are fixing up for Christmas. I think Christmas will be like all others to me. This time unless I will go to spend the with some little French Madamzell. The French girls are awful pretty and France is noted for plenty of wine and they come around with the bottle and gee, but that wine is fine. I am going to try to bring you a bottle with me. Father, I am going to send you a letter written from the boche*. I know you will laugh when you read it. Well Pa, as news is getting scarce I will have to stop for this time. Wishing you all a merry Christmas and a Happy New Year. Love and kisses to mother and sisters and you. Your loving son,

Private Clay P. Rankin
Co. D, 116th Infanttry,
American Expeditionary
Forces, France.

*The letter referred to will be found on another page of this issue of the Democrat.

Below will be found two interesting letters from Pvt. R. W. Teates to his parents at Beale-

IN MEMORIAM.

SUDDUTH.—In loving remembrance of my dear brother Corporal John D. Sudduth, Company D, 116th Infantry, who was killed in action seven months ago, aged 18 years.

Somewhere in the Argonne Forest,
  Far across the deep blue sea
Sleeps there within a silent grave,
  'One who is very dear to me.

Dearest John, how I miss you,
  This world will never know,
If tears could only bring you home,
  You would have been here long ago.

So now it's all over, 'over there,"
  And the world's great battle is over
Our dearest heroes now are marching
      home,
  But not my soldier brother.

Killed in action—that awful blow
  Has stamped my heart with pain
And every day it seems as though
  I look for you in vain.

Yes, in the great beyond some day,
  After my work on earth is over,
I will then stand face to face
  With my angel soldier brother.

1919   By his devoted sister, Eva.

237

Fairness • Openess • Honesty • Integrity

"I spend over 48 hours a week on the job as supervisor of Center District, in addition to my regular occupation making a living for my family. This is more than most people spend on their regular jobs. I also attend meetings of seven official committees to which I'm assigned. The sacrifice is worth it to make our quality of life better.

"I'm not owned by an influential special interest group wanting concessions for selfish reasons. Common citizens deserve a fair break.

"I've always served the people in my district with THEIR interests in mind. I'm an independent voice on the Board of Supervisors."

Who can you trust?
Someone who has stood with you through the years, or, someone who has not?

Jim Rankin
Center District Supervisor

Experience Makes a Difference! Stand with Jim Rankin on Nov. 3rd!

Authorized by James A. Rankin, Sr. (540) 345-0617

Paid Political Advertisement

E•D•U•C•A•T•I•O•N

Parents and Children can trust Jim Rankin when it comes to supporting our Public Schools...

Can we trust his opponent? No!

He promised the teachers that he's on their side but he wants to slash support to the schools by 10%.

From where do you think that money will come?

Teacher salaries and teacher positions, that's where!

Will your family's favorite teacher be here next year?

Jim Rankin

Center District Supervisor

Experience Makes a Difference!

Authorized by James A. Rankin, Sr., (540) 349-0617

RESOLUTION

A RESOLUTION PETITIONING THE VIRGINIA DEPARTMENT OF
TRANSPORTATION TO NAME THE MEETZE ROAD BRIDGE OVER U.S.
ROUTES 29 AND 17 IN HONOR OF U.S. ARMY PRIVATE FIRST CLASS CLAY
PRESTON RANKIN

WHEREAS, February 14, 2013, the Board of Supervisors, at the request of the
Fauquier County Veterans' Council, agreed to petition the Virginia Department of
Transportation (VDOT) for permission to name all bridges spanning primary and
secondary roads after military veterans; and

WHEREAS, the Fauquier County Veterans' Council has requested that the Board of
Supervisors now petition VDOT to name the Meetze Road Bridge the "Private First Class
Clay Preston Rankin, USA" Bridge; and

WHEREAS, on June 13, 1898, Clay Preston Rankin was born in Clifton Forge,
Virginia, and was a lifelong resident of Fauquier County; and

WHEREAS, Private First Class Rankin farmed and had several businesses in Fauquier
County and has two sons, a daughter and numerous grandchildren residing in Fauquier
County; and

WHEREAS, on July 25, 1917, Private First Class Rankin enlisted in the Army
National Guard; and

WHEREAS, Private First Class Rankin was awarded the Silver Star for displaying
remarkable courage and devotion in the front line through heavy machine gun fire; and

WHEREAS, Private First Class Rankin was also awarded the Italian War Cross for
gallantry in action while carrying important messages under enemy fire; and

WHEREAS, on May 29, 1919, Private First Class Rankin was honorably discharged from
and   duty;

WHEREAS, on September 15, 1967, Private First Class Rankin passed away; and

WHEREAS, the Board of Supervisors wishes to memorialize the life and sacrifice
of Private First Class Rankin; now, therefore, be it

RESOLVED by the Fauquier County Board of Supervisors this 13th day of November
2014, That the Board of Supervisors does hereby petition the Commonwealth Transportation
Board to name the Meetze Road Bridge the "Private First Class Clay Preston Rankin, USA"
Bridge.

241

242

FAUQUIER COUNTY BOARD OF SUPERVISORS
CENTER DISTRICT – 1923-2023

Edward W. Brown	1924-1931
Isham Keith	1932-1936
Thomas Frost	1936-1951
J. North Fletcher	1952-1959
James F. Austin	1960-1975
Robert L. Gilliam	1976-1979
Robert Keneflick	1980-1983
James F. Austin	1983
James Alvin Rankin, Sr.	1984-1991
James C. Bromfield	1992-1997
James Alvin Rankin, Sr.	1998
Joe Winkelmann	1998-2003
Richard W. Robinson	2004-2007
Terrence L. Nyhous	2008-2011
Christopher Granger	2012-2022
Kevin T. Carter	2022-Present

SOURCES

Chapter 1: Fauquier Famous

Francis Fauquier, The American Revolution, Colonial Williamsburg, www.ouramericanrevolution.org.

Toler, John, When Fauquier's Came to Town, *Fauquier Now,* February 22, 2022.

Life and Legacy of John Marshall, the Great Chief Justice, *The Fauquier Times,* March 21, 2019.

Profile: Governor William "Extra Billy" Smith, *The Fauquier Historical Society,* Winter 1987.

William "Extra Billy" Smith Brigade, *Gettysburg Daily,* May 20, 2008.

Coski, Ruth Ann, John Singleton Mosby, *Encyclopedia Virginia,* December 7, 2020.

Palmer, Isabelle S., Profile: Colonel John S. Mosby, *The Fauquier Historical Society*, Winter 1984.

Trexler, Edward Coleman, Capt. John Quincy Marr, Warrenton Rifles, *James River Valley Publishing*, 2010.

Chapter 2: Midland to Meuse-Argonne

Bosco, Peter, American At War, World War I, 1991, *Facts on File*, New York, New York.

Burg, David F. and Purcell, L. Edward, Almanac of World War I, *The University of Kentucky Press*, 1998.

Gilbert, Martin, The First World War, *Henry Holt and Company*, New York, 1994.

Willmott, H. P., World War I, *Dorling Kindersley Publishing, Inc.*, 2003.

Letter to Preston Baylor Rankin, Clay Rankin, Sergueant, France, *The Fauquier Democrat*, January 1919.

In Memoriam: John Suddduth, Eva Sudduth, *The Fauquier Democrat,* January 1919.

Cochrane, Raymond C., The Use of Gas in the Meuse-Argonne Campaign, *U.S. Army Chemical Corps Historical Studies,* Maryland 1958.

Toler, John, Vets Memorial to Honor Fauquier's Veterans War Dead, *The Times Democrat,* November 1991.

Chapter 3: Home on the Farm

Hot Air Cannot Stop Hard Times, *The Fauquier Democrat,* November 30, 1929.

Heinemann, Richard, Great Depression in Virginia, *Encyclopedia Virginia,* December 7, 2020.

Fast, Martha, Letter to First Lady Lou Henry Hoover, Iowa Department of Cultural Affairs, Herbert Hoover Presidential Library and Museum, January 3, 1931.

Clark, Mike, Hoover Prosperity, *The Fauquier Democrat,* March 18, 1931.

Toler, John, A Look Back at the History of Cinema in Warrenton, *The Fauquier Times,* February 5, 2017.

Chapter 4: Rakkasans

CSI Battlebook, The Battle of Sukchon-Sunchon, *Combat Studies Institute,* Fort Leavenworth, Kansas, 1966.

Ryder, Robert Randall, The Coldest Battle, American Legion, October 20, 2020.

Sgt. Deale Returns Home with Story of Korean War, *The Fauquier Democrat,* May 19, 1951.

War Threat Summary, *The Fauquier Democrat.* June 29, 1950.

Millett, Allan R., War Behind the Wire: Koje-do Prison Camp, *History Net,* January 20, 2009.

Marsh, George, What War is like in Korea: A Fauquier Sergeants Story: *The Fauquier Democrat,* April 3, 1952.

Toler, John, 50th Anniversary Commemoration of the Korean War, *The Fauquier Times,* June 21, 2000.

The Rakkasans, 187th "The Steel Berets," *Turner Publishing Company,* Paducah, Kentucky, 1991.

Chapter 5: Humble Public Servant

James A. Rankin, *The Fauquier Democrat,* May 10, 1983.

Campaign Flyer, For Supervisor: James A. Rankin, Center District, This is What I will work for Center District and Fauquier County.

These candidates are as concerned about your child's education as we are. Endorsement of Jim Rankin, Fauquier Education Association, 1983.

Voters For Jim Rankin, *The Fauquier Democrat,* November 15, 1983.

Fauquier County Board of Supervisors
Meeting Minutes,
www.fauquiercounty.gov.

School Bond Vote, *The Fauquier
Democrat,* March 5, 1987.

Hall, Arthur C. Rankin Critic Offers
Apology, *The Fauquier Democrat,* '
April 17, 1985.

Del Rosso, Donald, Center District: Rankin
believes he's served his people well," *The
Fauquier Democrat, April 23, 1987.*

Parker, Betsy Burke, Protecting
Fauquier's Future, *In Fauquier,*
October 25, 2021.

Blewitt, Mary K., Rankin Won't Seek
Center Board Seat, *The Times Democrat,*
May 9, 1991.

Lowrey, Dan, Vacant Seat to be Filled
Today, *The Times Democrat,* December
24, 1997.

Rankin Service Praised, *The Times
Democrat,* November 11, 1998.

Del Rosso, Don, Veteran vs. Rookie, *The Fauquier Citizen,* October 15, 1998.

Gulick, Edwin F., Auburn Dam: Good for County's Future, *The Fauquier Citizen,* October 19, 1998.

Shapira, Ian, Winkelmann Won't Seek Reelection, *The Washington Post,* March 6, 2003.

Chapter 6: Fauquier's Finest

Bosley, Linda, Old-Fashioned Service and Modern Inventory at Hometown Hardware, *The Fauquier Democrat,* January 15, 1987.

Chuse, David, Rankin's Hardware, *The Fauquier Magazine,* October 1991.

Lyne, David, Jim Rankin Builds Family Business Old-Fashioned Way, *Fauquier Now,* June 30, 2014.

Rittenour, Susette, Rankin's Hardware Celebrates 25 Years, *The Times Democrat,* April 18, 1991.

Rittenour, Susette, Jim Rankin Buys Waterloo Station, *The Fauquier Times,* June 11, 1992.

Del Russo, Partnership buys Waterloo Station from Jim Rankin for $8 million. *The Times Democrat,* April 2007.

Heincer, Amada, Rankin's Furniture Celebrates 25th Anniversary, *The Fauquier Times,* July 5, 2017.

Rankin's Furniture Warrenton, www.youtube.com, 2017.

The Best of Fauquier, *The Warrenton Lifestyle Magazine.*

Del Russo, Don, After 55 Years in Family, Rankin's Hardware Sold, *Fauquier Now,* March 30, 2021.

Winzeibert, David, Costello's ACE Hardware Add Three Virginia Stores, *Long Island Business News.*

Chapter 7: A Life Well Lived

Poe, Alan, NVL Night Baseball Games A Success So Far, *The Fauquier Democrat,* June 27, 1963.

Allen, Randal, Jim Rankin Earns 2015 Good Scout Award, *The Fauquier Times,* September 29, 2015.

Scouting Award to Honor the Late Roland Tapscott, *Fauquier Now,* September 29, 2014.

Certificate of Appreciation, The Honorable Robert Gates, United States Secretary of Defense.

Jim Rankin Builds Family Business Old-Fashioned Way, *Fauquier Now.*

Bosley, Linda, Old-Fashioned Service and Modern Inventory at Hometown Hardwares, *The Fauquier Democrat,* January 15, 1987.

About the Author

Harry Frederick Burroughs III was born in Riverhead, New York. He began his career in the U.S. House of Representatives on May 16, 1977. For the next 37 years, he worked for six members of Congress, served as Republican Chief of Staff of the House Merchant Marine and Fisheries Committee and the Staff Director of the House Natural Resources Subcommittee on Fisheries, Wildlife, Oceans, and Insular Affairs.

Since retiring in 2015, Harry has written a number of books including *My Life on Capitol Hill, The People's Sheriff, A Century of Keeping the Peace and Justice Delayed, Justice Denied: The Tragic Story of Harris Neck, Georgia.* The author lives with his wife, Gayle in Warrenton, Virginia.

Rankin's Place: A Story of a Hero and Community Leader is a fascinating biography of James Alvin Rankin, Sr., a man who is a living legend in his beloved Fauquier County, Virginia. His story is a modern day version of one of Horatio Alger's "Rages to Riches" tales. Jim Rankin grew up on a leased farm during the worst economic depression in our nation's history. His family may have been dirt-poor farmers but Jim understood he could live the American Dream through courage, determination, hard work, honesty and perservance.

Jim Rankin first joined the United States Army at 17-years-old. He was a proud member of the 187th Airborne who fought blood battles under the harshest conditions throughout the Korean Peninsula. When these battles were won, the 187th Rakkasans were sent to put down the riots occurring at the Koje-do POW Camps. Like his father, Jim Rankin felt it was his obligation to service his country. He was a real life paratrooper who rose from a Private to Staff Sergeant in less than 11 months.

In 1983, Jim Rankin decided he wanted to be an independent voice for the people of Fauquier County. For nine years, he was the Center District Representative on the Fauquier County Board of Supervisors. He was beholden to the people who elected him and not a single special interest group. His principles were always fairness, openness, honesty and integrity.

He was an outstanding representative who voted to improve the lives of his constituents and protect the rural agricultural beauty of Fauquier County.

In 1966, Jim Rankin opened his first True Value Hardware Store. Over the next 57 years, his family owned Business Empire expanded to include hardware stores in Colonial Beach, King George and Winchester, Virginia. His current store, Rankin's Furniture celebrated its 32th year in business. Each of these stores offered quality products, outstanding customer service and great prices. Rankin's stores have been the one-stop shop for thousands of happy consumers who have consistently voted them the "Best of Fauquier County" and "The Readers Choice."

Jim Rankin is also a generous benefactor for a multitude of organizations and has always been willing to give a helping hand to those in need. As a humble man, he rarely speaks of his contributions or willingness to help. Nevertheless, he has made the difference in the lives of so many people in Fauquier County. James Alvin Rankin, Sr. is a hero, patriot, public servant and a Hall of Fame small businessman. This is his incredible life story and it is a remarkable one!

Made in the USA
Monee, IL
31 January 2024

51951498R00144